PRIVATE
NEW YORK

REMARKABLE

PRIVATE
NEW YORK

RESIDENCES

TEXT BY
CHIPPY IRVINE

PHOTOGRAPHY BY
ALEX McLEAN

ABBEVILLE PRESS
PUBLISHERS
NEW YORK

Editor: Jacqueline Decter
Designer: Julie Rauer
Copy Chief: Robin James
Production Manager: Dana Cole

P. 157: "On Your Toes" (Richard Rodgers, Lorenz Hart) © 1936 Chappell & Co., Inc.
(Renewed). All rights reserved. Used by permission.
FRONT COVER: Library of a Fifth Avenue apartment.
BACK COVER: Living room of Hans Peter Weiss's SoHo loft.
FRONTISPIECE: Living room of Kenneth Jay Lane's Murray Hill apartment.
DEDICATION PAGE: Detail of the living room in Maxime de La Falaise's Fifth Avenue loft.
P. 9: Detail of the living room in Stephen and Cathy Graham's Upper East Side town house.

First edition

Library of Congress Cataloging-in-Publication Data

Irvine, Chippy.
Private New York : remarkable residences / texts by Chippy Irvine : photography by
Alex McLean.
p. cm.
Includes bibliographical references.
ISBN 1-55859-106-0
1. Interior decoration—New York (N.Y.)—History—20th century.
I. Title.
NK2004.I78 1990
747.2147'1—dc20
90-268
CIP

Printed and bound in Italy

For my sister, Kitty Grime

C O N T

ENTS

PREFACE

Ever since I arrived in New York from England some thirty years ago, I've considered it an energetic, captivating city, a magnet for the talented and a haven for the prosperous. While working on this book I have explored places on and off the city's beaten track, discovering along the way a variety of fascinating people and unexpected dwellings. Included here are such diverse and alluring residences of the affluent as a town house on Carnegie Hill, a penthouse on Park Avenue, and a luxurious Fifth Avenue apartment. Juxtaposed, New York style, are a tiny, imaginative one-roomer in Greenwich Village and a fantastic but certainly not lavish houseboat on the Hudson. The often unfairly neglected boroughs yielded some unusual finds—a remarkably preserved Gothic Revival house on Staten Island, an artist's studio in Brooklyn's Clinton Hill area, and a trove of Biedermeier in a Brooklyn Heights apartment. A house in Harlem depicts the grandeur of the Convent Avenue area. Another current facet of New York's residential scene—the loft—is represented by fine examples in several neighborhoods, including TriBeCa, SoHo, Ladies' Mile, and even Fifth Avenue. Furnishings range from well-bred eighteenth-century English suites to pure Salvation Army "junque," with many stops in between.

To retain authenticity, photographer Alex McLean used natural, available light wherever possible. Rooms were not elaborately styled for the pictures and we did not bring in truckloads of flowers or accessories. Instead, the residences are depicted just as their owners live in them.

EAST SIDE STYLE AND GRACE

Manhattan! The name resonates with the promise of glamour and luxury. Anne Bass's apartment in a building on the Upper East Side, facing the green expanse of Central Park, is without doubt one of the best examples of a truly deluxe residence.

The building was designed by Rosario Candela, an architect fancied by New York's affluent cliff dwellers, in partnership with Warren and Wetmore—the architects of Grand Central Terminal. Commissioned by developer/builder Anthony Campegna, a fellow Italian who had worked with Candela on previous projects, the building was far grander than either had previously produced. Described by the *New York Times* as "12 mansions built one on top of another," it was completed in 1929 as a cooperative building in which prospective purchasers could buy large amounts of space and have them custom designed. The building has always been occupied by the wealthy and, as Paul Goldberger points out in *New York: The City Observed*, its residents "managed to avoid the problem of deciding whether one of the great, formal iron marquees of old or a newfangled canvas canopy is the better thing to have—they have always had both, one fitting neatly under the other."

As an overture to the rest of the apartment, the elevator lobby sets the tone. Its floor is inlaid with polished white, gray, and black marble, echoed on the walls by exquisitely executed faux marble panels punctuated by faux Ionic pilasters. A monopodium marble side table holds a Nancy Graves bronze sculpture in the shape of a blithely painted, fantastical lyre strung with pink fish and set on a piece of broken column. This sculpture was particularly enticing to Mrs. Bass because a lyre motif is the logo of the New York City Ballet and she is not only an ardent balletomane but a major fundraiser for the ballet company.

The workmanship in this tiny lobby is of such impeccable quality it is obvious that exceptional taste and expertise were involved. For four years decorator Mark Hampton worked with Anne Bass, tempering her strong love of pared-down contemporary design with his knowledge of architectural history, to achieve her ideal and very stylish residence.

In the main entrance hall, the walls and doors are lacquered in Dior-chic gray with panels crisply picked out in white. Immediately facing the entrance is a daydreamy painting of a young girl gazing out of a window by Polish-French artist Balthus. Guarding the door leading to the drawing room is one of the six original bronze casts of Degas's *La Petite danseuse de quatorze ans*, the subject's hair tied back with a white satin bow. In all the main reception rooms—hall, library, living room, and dining room—the rich patina of antique *parquet de Versailles* covers the floors.

One is lured into the large drawing room by two vivid, red-hued Rothko paintings on the far wall. Their intense glow is set off by the cream-colored background and furniture, all anchored on a flower-entwined 1770 Axminster carpet. The grand scale and style of a suite of George II sofas and armchairs and a set of George III oval-backed armchairs are restrained by cream upholstery in varying weaves of silk, or silk combined with linen—only natural fibers are used throughout the apartment—and the once-brilliant gilt on the gessoed frames has been softened to a subtle hint. A Charles II bench has been remarkably modernized by a cream seat covering. Similarly, two Charles II silvered and fancifully carved cabinets with cupids, flowers,

Two tables are set for dinner in the mirrored dining room. The circular faux marble tables hold a variety of silver candlesticks, iridescent stemware, and embroidered napery. The Mies van der Rohe chrome-framed chairs are upholstered in cream fabric. Over the green-and-white marble fireplace is Monet's *Houses of Parliament*, and between the windows is his *Peupliers de l'automne*. The carpet, made in London, is a rare silk-and-wool Pontremoli with a border of dolphins and birds.

and shells sit comfortably beneath the austere horizontal stripes of the two Agnes Martin paintings flanking the fireplace. In pride of place is another Balthus, *Les Trois soeurs*, 1966. The tall windows are not curtained. Instead, interior shutters of mirror glass have been ingeniously engineered to fill the window recesses, reflecting light and doubling the width of the window. When shuttered, the mirrors make the already generously sized room look twice as big. In the summer, when the sun pours in, electronically operated sun shields can be lowered. Each window recess is fitted with a cream-colored padded cushion. Centered between the four windows is Degas's *Femme en peignoir bleu, le torse découvert*, 1887–90, and between the windows flanking it are handsome silvered-iron Louis XIV torchères, believed to have come from the gardens at Versailles. Found in Paris, these torchères, which now support pots of plants or vases of flowers, were Anne Bass's first purchase for the apartment. In one corner of the room a grand piano stands near a Morris Louis painting—one in his Veils series. In another corner is a gilt-and-lacquered round wood table, its top inlaid with Japanese Export porcelain. On it are displayed handsomely tooled and bound volumes, including several on the Russian ballet set designer Léon Bakst. A third corner contains a demi-lune, marble-topped bureau on which is a folio of George Brookshaw's *Illustrated Fruits of England*. Lighting, controlled by a battery of switches, is cleverly concealed in ceiling spotlights set into a recessed rectangular strip

A Monet painting, *Houses of Parliament*, its glowing red sun repeating the radiant colors of the Rothkos, entices one into the dining room. The pale green–and–white marble mantelpiece came with the apartment, and the rare, signed Pontremoli neoclassic silk-and-wool carpet, with its central medallion, vines, and border of dolphins and birds, fits the room miraculously both in color and size. A split pediment was added above the door opposite the fireplace, which is reflected in the overmantel mirror, giving the room architectural balance. An inspired idea was to set mirrors in the molded wall panels and, in addition, to bevel the mirror edges, imparting an unusual, faceted-jewel quality to the glass. On these mirrors are hung two other paintings by Monet, their lightly gilded wood frames inset with thin bands of mirror glass, which make the paintings seem to float. Their colors echo the soft, but by no means soppy or girlish, greens and pinks found in the carpet. For dinner parties, one, two, or even four tables can be set. These round tables are painted in pale faux marble lacquer and surrounded by Mies van der Rohe chrome-framed Brno chairs, unconventionally upholstered in cream fabric. The table mats and napkins are embroidered with delicate flowers. Iridescent bubble-shaped goblets echo the prism-formed rainbows that bounce off the beveled glass on the walls. Sixty-six tiny recessed

In the elevator lobby, the three-toned marble floor is echoed by faux marble pilastered walls. On a marble table is Nancy Graves's *Lyra*, 1983.

The architectural details of the library were already in place when Mrs. Bass moved in, but the dark paneling has been lightened with subtle, two-tone paint work, outlined in white. Between the arched bookcases is an English George III pier mirror. Four George II library chairs are covered in a striped-and-flowered French silk, which blends with the nineteenth-century needlepoint carpet.

The powder room, lined in silver leaf, is reminiscent of a tea chest. On one wall is a Florentine costume design by Stefano della Bella, 1661. The tufted seat is upholstered in gray moiré. A bowl of pale pink roses on a Venetian table is reflected in the mirror.

lights on the ceiling are reflected in the mirrors and glow like stars. The effect is almost like being in a limpid, glassy green pool.

Beyond the dining room are the butler's pantry, kitchen, linen rooms, and staff rooms. This area was completely gutted and renovated. Pristine white glass-fronted cupboards and Corian counters line the almost clinically organized space.

Off the entrance hall is the library, which was paneled in dark wood when the apartment belonged to the art-collecting Paysons. Mrs. Bass has kept the room's four arched bookcases, now filled with leather-bound volumes; the inlaid marble fireplace; and two bookcases ingeniously concealed behind huge panels that swing open but can also be used to display art. But she and Mark Hampton agreed that the room should be lightened, so it was glazed and stippled in two delicate, neutral shades, with sharp white emphasizing the molding. A George III pier mirror was found for the mantel, and a French striped silk damask that blends perfectly with the nineteenth-century English gros point carpet was used to upholster four substantial George II carved wood library armchairs from a suite made for St. Giles, the Earl of Shaftsbury's house. Over a George III mahogany library writing table where Mrs. Bass handles much of her correspondence hangs Picasso's *Leçon de dessin*, 1925. Plain, off-white silk curtains hang from a simple curtain rod, softening the windows and breaking into elegant folds on the

A suite of George II furniture and a set of oval-backed George III parcel gilt armchairs are upholstered in a variety of cream-colored silk fabrics. The carpet is an eighteenth-century Axminster. On the far wall is a Morris Louis painting from his Veils series. Beneath it is a Charles II carved bench. To the left is a 1983 Agnes Martin painting. The small carved table near it is also Charles II. Over the fireplace is Balthus's *Les Trois soeurs*. The window insets are tall, mirrored shutters.

The gray-and-white lacquered entrance hall is adorned with Balthus's *Jeune fille à la fenêtre*, 1955, and *La Petite danseuse de quatorze ans* by Degas. In the drawing room is Rothko's *Number 1*, 1962.

floor. A large and witty Nancy Graves tree-shaped sculpture, *Medusa*, prevents the room from verging on the academic.

A door on the opposite side of the hall leads to a jewel box of a powder room. The walls of both the anteroom and toilet are lined in laid-on silver leaf, with parts of the molded panels overlaid in a darker steel color. Framed early dance costume drawings—one a 1661 Florentine drawing, the other a Louis XIII drawing—flank the looking glass. A tufted slipper seat is upholstered and skirted with pewter gray silk moiré, which also skirts the washbasin. Jim Dine prints of the Venus di Milo decorate the walls of the toilet.

A step leads up into the family's more private

quarters. The focus of Anne Bass's bedroom is her four-poster, luxuriously swagged with gray silk taffeta, held in place with beribboned taffeta *choux*. Her bathroom is a veritable *salon de glace* of infinite reflections. Bedrooms and bathrooms for her two daughters and for guests are also found in this wing.

The success of the apartment is due primarily to the handling of wonderful antique English furniture in a contemporary, uninhibited, easy way—there is nothing to beat the combination of good English furniture and impeccably efficient American housekeeping! The apartment reflects the style and taste of its owner and her decorator, and extends the tradition set by the late influential decorator Billy Baldwin. It is also very New York!

CAST-IRON SCULPTURAL LOFT

A unique contribution to architecture can be found in New York's cast-iron districts. One of these districts is in TriBeCa (short for Triangle Below Canal Street) and the other is in an area dubbed SoHo (for South of Houston Street).

In the 1850s, when Italianate details were being cultivated in New York's brownstones, a handful of engineers began applying the Italianate style to this new, American, and principally New York City form of architecture. Technical breakthroughs—which exuberantly often overtook aesthetic considerations—allowed cast-iron architecture to become popular as an inexpensive means of reproducing fancy detailing previously possible only in stone. To quote the American Institute of Architects' *AIA Guide to New York City* by White and Willensky, "More Corinthian, Ionic, Doric, Composite, Egyptian and *Lord-knows-what-else* columns were cast for New York facades in the 1850s and 1860s than Greece and Rome turned out in a thousand years."

The TriBeCa Cast-Iron District is full of generously scaled loft buildings with facades fashioned from separate sections of prefabricated molded iron assembled on-site. This method not only was cheaper and less cumbersome than dealing with carved stone but also required less time and skill. In addition, cast iron was a relatively light yet sound material, which made large windows and strong, slender columns possible. Substantial buildings could be supported on interior cast-iron columns that became leaner as they reached the upper floors. These skinny-looking pillars gave distinctive new proportions to the buildings constructed at this time in Manhattan.

Cast iron lent itself to the Italian style. Architectural critics have compared Manhattan's cast-iron era to sixteenth-century Venice, another city where large buildings were erected on small sites because of land limitation. Similarly, the often gloomy New York winters—comparable to those of Venice—made it desirable to let as much light as possible in through windows.

New York's cast-iron buildings have traditionally served as warehouses or factories for light industry, but are increasingly being used as artists' studios and residences. With the growing success of many New York–based artists, lofts have been extensively renovated in collaboration with serious and gifted architects.

White Street is fairly typical of the TriBeCa area. The street was named in 1762 after Captain Thomas White, who settled in New York, bought property, became a wealthy importer of tea, and gained prominence in public affairs. After his death—or so the story goes, according to James Ludwig's *Alphabet of Greatness*, a typewritten book in the local history section of the New York Public Library—the captain's two spinster daughters developed a passion for everything white: they chose as their estate administrator a Mr. White (no relation); they dressed in white; every stick of their furniture was white; and, when White Street was opened, they lived there in a white house. The street now contains a mixture of styles. Near West Broadway, builder Gideon Tucker's two-story house with attic dormers, belonging more to the eighteenth than the nineteenth century, survives miraculously amid robust, Corinthian-columned cast-iron structures. In a more typical loft building, contemporary sculptor Bryan Hunt owns a studio and duplex living loft that has been masterfully designed with the help of David Piscuskas and Walter Chatham of the firm 1100 Architects.

Industrial metal stairs ascend from the fifth-floor workroom to the bedroom floor. On the storage drawers is Hunt's *Jawbone Lake*. The drawing above it is a study for a piece called *The Navigator*. In front of the staircase is *Pilgrim*, a figure on a journey, with a golden face. On the wall by the stairs is a photograph by Swiss photographer Steiner.

Hunt was born in Terre Haute, Indiana, was educated in Los Angeles, and has exhibited all over the world, but he has chosen to live and work in New York. The painter and real estate agent Jan Hashey advised him to look at a loft in TriBeCa, and he found it by riding around the area on his bike. As soon as he saw the space, previously a textile warehouse, Hunt knew it was right for him, and he was the first artist to move into the building. Brownstone steps lead up to a typical warehouse entrance. The ground floor is Hunt's studio. The basement below is used as a workshop and as a storeroom for large pieces of sculpture, some of which are laid in rows on the floor, carefully wrapped like mummies. The studio itself is impressive in height and size. Slender structural columns, reaching

up to the pressed-metal ceiling, divide the space majestically. Near the entrance, an office harbors today's indispensables, including a bike and a computer and fax machine for his secretary. Conference areas can be partitioned off with curtains. Works-in-progress are placed in this abundant space with a deliberation that influences even the way tools are laid out on the worktable. Light floods in during part of the day and at night the studio can be lit by spotlights on the ceiling.

A warehouse elevator ascends to Hunt's loft apartment on the fifth floor, passing painter David Salle's studio en route. Both artists belong to the generation of contemporary and influential American artists that includes Eric Fischl, Bill Jensen, Robert Moscovitz, Susan Rothenberg, Kenny Scharf, Julian

In the ground-floor studio the textile warehouse's original slender cast-iron columns and pressed-metal ceiling were retained. Though the far window is blocked off, a skylight provides necessary daylight. Tools are organized on a table in the foreground.

A bathroom on the fifth floor divides the living room and the workroom. A shelf over the sink holds a Spanish landscape by Bryan Hunt. The Gemini lamp with a shelf to display small objects was designed by Hunt. The figure is a tiny sculpture found in Nepal.

In the dining area the wood-topped, steel-based table was designed by Hunt and is made in limited edition by A/D Gallery, New York. The candlesticks were also designed by Hunt and made in a limited edition by Gemini G.E.L. Four black and two natural-colored Eames molded plywood chairs surround the table. A black lacquer Alvar Aalto table by the wall on the right sits below an Eric Fischl painting of an amorphous child in a ballet tutu. Various objects on the shelves include an antique Japanese falcon and a French articulated wooden horse model used by artists. On the wall at far left is Hunt's *Great Wall of China. (overleaf)*

Schnabel, Donald Sultan, and the late Keith Haring.

Hunt's living area is described by Chatham as "tough" and "sculptural." Various elements have been blended to fill the large space without losing its loftlike integrity. Original heating pipes are left in place, as is the ceiling of pressed-metal squares, typical of these lofts. Newly laid wood floors are broken up by large, unfinished terra-cotta tiles and slabs of stone. The main floor is divided into two basic sections by a large bathroom that includes an open shower and by an industrial metal staircase with grid landings and steps held in place by rugged nuts and bolts. The first section is a workroom with an elongated worktable running along one wall. Below it are huge, white-knobbed storage drawers for drawings and large sheets of paper. An exercise bike and a rowing machine are in evidence. The second section is the living area, which includes a space—defined by a subtle carpet from western Persia—filled with comfortable black leather-covered 1940s sofas, chairs, and ottomans. Built into one wall are bookshelves and a low stone shelf into which a fireplace is set. Logs are stored in a concealed cupboard close by. The dining area is near an open-plan, gray-and-white-painted kitchen with butcher-block counters. All the furniture is in the twentieth-century classic architect-designed category. So much sun streams in that Hunt likes to spend some of his daytime hours on this floor. Upstairs, a penthouse suite, consisting of bedroom, bathroom, and terrace, was built for Hunt onto the original roof. Glass doors leading onto the terrace are set in steel frames with handsomely designed hardware. A cedar fence surrounding the terrace opens amusingly to disclose the vista of the street below.

Throughout the loft one is mesmerized by Hunt's strategically placed sculpture. An ethereal gilded dirigible, one of his series of Airships cunningly fashioned from wood and silk, kisses the wall above one's head. The midsection of these eighteen-sided airships is echoed by the eighteen-sided bases Hunt uses for his standing sculptures. Pieces from a 1974 series based on great monuments include *Tower of Babel* in the work section; *Odeon,* 1977, placed between two windows; and *Great Wall of China,* which at certain times of the day throws dragon-shaped shadows on a wall in the living room. Other series include pools of cast bronze called Lakes, meteorlike chunks called Quarries, and gushing cascades with human overtones that he names Falls. Hunt's witty and sensitive hand

The penthouse bedroom leads out onto a terrace. Sheets and buttoned-down pillow cases are of striped oxford cotton. A palm peeps from behind a shoji screen. Above the bed a slender, ancient Thai Buddha stands on one of Bryan Hunt's eighteen-sided bases. The dog, Chet (after Baker), sits on a Chinese rug. A kimono covers a bedside chair, Chet's usual sleeping place.

The terrace is fenced all around but a door opens onto a vista of Franklin Street. A Hunt piece, *Daphne*, is an abstract figure of the nymph changing into a tree. The terrace garden contains a crabapple tree, tomatoes, and hot peppers, and an herb garden that includes parsley, coriander, sage, and rosemary.

is revealed in his drawings and his discerning eye in his black-and-white photographs. In addition, one finds innovative lighting fixtures he has designed. A glass-topped torchère set on a bulging metal stand that splays out at the bottom is a standard lamp produced in limited edition with Gemini G.E.L. gallery. The same firm makes Hunt's candlesticks and the reading lamps with perforated

copper shades near the living room sofas. The dining room table, produced by A/D Gallery, is another of Hunt's pieces.

A versatile designer, photographer, and artist, Bryan Hunt seems to have selected cast metal as his current medium. How very suitable, then, that he chose this Cast-Iron District as his habitat.

ANTIQUE GLASS IN GREENWICH VILLAGE

In 1968 art consultant Wade McCann exchanged the wide-open spaces of his native Texas for a tiny, tightly packed apartment in New York's Greenwich Village. Over the years he has filled it with an erudite accumulation of treasures, which include antique silver, ceramics, lamps, furniture, pictures, and, especially, glass. Though of sober mien himself, he admits a fascination with rare artifacts that relate to serious drinking!

Collecting comes easily—and naturally—to him. As a museum curator and adviser to the New-York Historical Society and to private collectors, he has access to the latest—or earliest—scholarly knowledge. An even more powerful influence was his family, all of whom were collectors of one kind or another. His father collected clocks and guns; his mother accumulated Queen Anne and William and Mary furniture, though recently she, too, has begun acquiring glass and is knowledgeable about antique ceramics. His two older sisters search for kitchen antiques such as graniteware (mottled gray enamel on tin) and cooking utensils from the turn of the century. Even his niece looks out for affordable collectibles such as Depression glass and Fiesta ware.

With his sensitivity to history, McCann's choice of an apartment in Greenwich Village made sense. The Village preserves a feeling of history, rare in a city that deliberately prefers to tear down the old in order to build ever higher, more dehumanized buildings. Of all New York's neighborhoods, it has retained, with a struggle, much of its attractive, picturesque quality. The story of the Village goes back to a time when the Manahatin Indians called the area Sappokanican. During the days of Dutch

supremacy, the second director-general of New Netherland acquired the area north of Canal Street, naming it Bossen Bouwerie. He made money growing tobacco on his farm there. After England took over in 1664, the area gradually became known as the Green Village, and in 1713 city records officially referred to it as Greenwich Village. Country seats were maintained there by affluent colonists, the most prominent being an Irish officer in the English navy, Sir Peter Warren, who, in 1733, bought 300 acres.

After the Revolution prosperous tradesmen, followed by merchants and bankers, moved to the Village, using it as a rural retreat from the hustle and bustle of the city, which was then expanding north from Wall Street. By the 1790s streets were being laid out, following well-established routes such as Skinner Road (present-day Christopher Street), Greenwich Lane (now Greenwich Avenue), and Greenwich Street.

The main impetus to the growth of the Village was a series of fever outbreaks in the city during the early nineteenth century. Greenwich Village was considered healthier because of its higher elevation, good natural drainage, and minimal exposure to ship-transported tropical diseases.

One of the earliest thoroughfares in the Village was the street now known as Waverly Place. A "pleasantly Classical street" is how Norval White and Elliot Willensky describe it in the *AIA Guide to New York City*. It extends east and west from Washington Square North, and its western branch angles north at Christopher Street. Before 1833 it was called Sixth Street, but was renamed Waverly Place in response to a petition from admirers of Sir Walter Scott—author of the Waverley novels—

On the mantelpiece in the living room is a pair of Empire gilt Argand lamps with Gothic motifs. The French candlesticks are mid-eighteenth-century silvered brass, a finish that predates Sheffield plating. The tortoiseshell looking glass is Queen Anne, 1680–1710. The Gothic Revival French clock is Charles X, circa 1830. Two spill vases were made by a competitor of the Wedgwood factory, 1815. The pair of Derby dessert plates showing Italian scenes was made in 1805. The glittery glass Christmas tree and a rhinestone brooch that was found in the street add a bit of kitsch.

who died in 1832.

Wade McCann resides on Waverly Place in one of three identical, adjacent houses. Though the street boasts houses of an earlier date, these three blend in unobtrusively. Built in 1892 of brick, with ashlar (square stone facings) on the first floor, they are each five stories high, designed in the Italian Renaissance style, their entrances embellished with pediments set on short columns. The first owner was J. H. Luhrs; the architect was Edward L. Angell. Like much of the nineteenth-century building in the Village they were originally intended to be inexpensive rooming houses with small, self-contained apartments crammed in. Each apartment was equipped with an indoor bathroom, complete with a diminutive bathtub. McCann had his eye on one of the last of those early tubs and had even restored his own bathroom around the hope of acquiring it, but to his dismay there was nothing he could do to prevent the tub from being callously smashed up in the course of Formica-encased "improvements" on a recently vacated apartment. Unfortunately, short-sighted and insensitive landlords are often slow to catch on to the growing preservation movement. If they were to preserve original architecture and detailing, their investments would be far more appealing and lucrative.

With the advice and support of local landmarks historian Regina Kellerman, McCann has tried to salvage much original detailing, only to be censured by the owner for being "a nuisance."

Through his research McCann discovered that the apartment's original occupant—who lived there for forty-five years—was a member of the Ritz Brothers, a renowned team of circus gymnasts. The location was at a convenient distance from the then busy and fashionable thoroughfare of 14th Street where the Ritz Brothers often performed.

Inside the apartment, myriad layers of hard-to-remove paint still veil woodwork, moldings, and the once clear glass lights above the doors. Nevertheless, by judicious selection of paint color (predominantly a rich dark green), much of the original atmosphere has been retained. Existing details, such as the fancy rosettes on the door and window corners, have been preserved. McCann collects pieces of original molding that are pitched out of other apartments when they are being modernized and uses them to restore his own. Even the original gas line leading to the light in the kitchen is still visible.

It is the owner's collections, however—ingen-

A collection of antique glass decanters, tumblers, and silver bottle tickets are crowded on a shelf in the kitchen.

Every shelf, cupboard, and wall space in the minute kitchen is filled with a melange of champagne glasses, punch cups, Anglo-Irish Georgian decanters, American glass made in the Pittsburgh area, early-nineteenth-century English ceramics, pickle jars, cut-glass plates, and so on. A 1900 electric lamp by the window is by Hawkes & Co., Corning, New York.

iously shoehorned onto shelves, assembled into tablescapes, arranged in artistic piles, plastered on walls, and perched on chairs—that make this apartment such a fascinating magpie's nest. Various themes are evident. Rare—because of their fragility—champagne goblets fill one shelf. Much sought-after silver bottle tickets read "Madeira," "Claret," "Whiskey," "Gin," "Champagne," or "Port." McCann also collects ice pitchers; one has a glass side pocket to hold cooling pieces of ice without weakening the drink. Tantalus sets—decanters in

trios, literally "to tempt"—are relics of men's smoking rooms; McCann owns one set that came from an early Rolls-Royce. Many styles of lighting were devised during the nineteenth century, and McCann's collection contains rare examples. Glass and gilt-bronze nineteenth-century Argand lamps, first used in France, then England, and retailed in New York, were invented by the Swiss scientist Emile Argand. They work on the principle of the gravity flow of oil. Sconces, candlesticks, and candelabra share space with adapted nineteenth-century solar

Above the American Federal 1815 mirror in the dining/living room is a rare Jeffreys Hamett O'Neale Chelsea plate with an Aesop's-fable border, 1755. Below is a fine piece of Derby armorial porcelain from a dessert service. On the windowsills are solar lamps by Cornelius & Co., Philadelphia. The English sconces and candelabra, 1820s, are of a type commonly used in American interiors of the period. Modern furnishings include a basic oatmeal-colored sofa. Winter-blooming cyclamen and hanging Christmas cactus (*Zygocactus*) from Mexico soften the windows in place of curtains. *(left)*

The walls of the tiny bedroom are hung with pictures. The ship painting is *The Commodore Bateman*, by Clement Freitag, circa 1860. The large eighteenth-century print depicts William Penn's *Treaty with the Indians* after the painting by Benjamin West. A series of 1750s engravings shows famous English castles, none of which, alas, is extant, for the stones have long since been stolen by local farmers to build their own houses and barns.

A kitchen shelf shows a collection of rare Liverpool Transfer–printed creamware with images of George Washington. Depictions of Washington are often paired with the marquis de Lafayette or Benjamin Franklin. A small punch bowl depicts all three, while the jug shows Washington and a Boston ship, the *Mary Ann*, on the back. The small coffee cup has the marquis on the reverse.

lamps and early electric lights. One of McCann's favorite possessions is his dining room tablecloth, which was embroidered in drawnwork by his grandfather. In Texas at that time it was not unusual for men and boys to do stitchwork. Made from a flour sack, it still bears the almost-washed-off brand name, Red Top, on the back.

All of the rare and unusual pieces in the apartment are documented and lovingly cared for by the owner.

PARK AVENUE TRADITIONAL

Architecturally aware—and affluent—New Yorkers play the Rosario Candela game. His name pops up endlessly in discussions about New York's "good" apartment buildings. He was the architect of the city's grandest apartment houses when really imposing apartments were being built in the 1920s and 1930s.

Candela started life humbly. According to Christopher Gray in a *New York Times* article, he was born in Palermo, Sicily, in 1890, the son of a plasterer. He emigrated to the United States in his early twenties, at which time he spoke very little English. Even so, he entered Columbia University, where he showed exceptional talent and received his Certificate of Architecture in 1915. At first he worked as a draftsman for Gaetano Ajello, also from Palermo, then for Frederick S. Sterner. In 1920 he hung out his own shingle and by 1922 his first building, with baroque-style detailing, was erected on the northeast corner of 92nd Street and Broadway. The builder was Anthony Campegna, one of several Italian-born developers with whom Candela became affiliated.

Many of his earliest designs were tall apartment buildings on Riverside Drive and West End, Park, and Fifth avenues. From 1927 on, his work was in the superluxury class, and he was a master at providing what his rich and discriminating clientele required. This might include separate private laundries, vaults, or a room where garbage pails could be cleaned with steam. His trademark, apart from the sheer size of the apartments he planned with such care, was his regard for privacy as an attribute of good living. Kitchens and bathrooms never opened onto living rooms. The living quarters, the sleeping quarters, and the service quarters were all kept separate. As the exteriors of the buildings were completed, interiors would be individually customized for buyers, who often commissioned Candela to design them as well.

One couple—a lawyer with a large corporate law firm, and his wife, the executive assistant for a prominent businesswoman—live in a traditionally furnished apartment in the most luxurious of Candela's early apartment houses. Built in 1926, it was a novel blend of maisonettes with separate entrances, duplexes, a triplex, and one-floor apartments. The lower part of the building includes stone-carved detailing of superior quality, and to this day the building retains an aristocratic atmosphere. Built for developer Michael Paterno, each apartment had a minimum of two closets per bedroom; fireplaces in every library, living room, and dining room; a wine cellar opening off each dining room; and a 650-square-foot living room. The apartments have remained the same size as they were in the original plan. The couple occupies one of the building's single-floor apartments, which provides them and their schnauzer, Spats, with ample space.

Though decorated in a manner that Candela would have understood—and that would not be out of place in an A. R. Gurney play—when they first bought it, a few architectural changes had to be made. The kitchen, always the first room to be outdated in our technological age, required complete renovation. What had been a butler's pantry and small kitchen were opened up into one large, sunny room. Old and oxidized kitchen units were replaced with spanking-new facilities. Neither husband nor wife is a fanatical cook, so there was no need for

In the completely renovated kitchen white tiles have been enlivened with heraldic tiles found in Siena. Matching plates and carafe are used for breakfast. A sunny awning was added to complement the flower boxes. The framed pictures are of French bistros.

elaborate stoves and extra burners beloved by the high-tech kitchen set. For dinner parties, food is either prepared ahead of time or catered, the object being to spend time with friends, not slave in the kitchen. They both liked the idea of window boxes full of bright flowers but the structure of the building made it impossible to install them outside. Having decided to bring them indoors, they deemed it logical to hang vivid striped awnings inside, too, though the awning man had a hard time understanding this. Heraldic tiles found in Siena, Italy, were incorporated into the plain white tiling on some of the walls and counters. Similar heraldic designs appear on the breakfast plates and carafes used in the kitchen for casual meals.

The couple already owned good family furniture and portraits. The wife inherited a historic farm in Connecticut. Their New York apartment has benefited from this genuine—and refreshing—family heritage. It was after visiting the farm as a Harvard law student that the lawyer first became interested in antique furniture; the impeccable American furniture of its main house attracted him. He and his wife began collecting eighteenth-century furniture, and their interests then broadened to include nineteenth-century American paintings, their principal collecting interest today.

The previous owner had decorated the dining room with a celadon-toned Chinese wallpaper from New York Orientalia specialists Charles R. Gracie & Sons. As the wallpaper was in excellent condition and very much to the couple's taste, it was protected throughout the renovations and restored where necessary, especially in the spot where a pair of handsome antique doors was installed. These replaced an arch similar to the one in the marble hall that opens into the living room. A chandelier in the dining room was also retained. Crown moldings, however, underwent alteration with the addition of a row of lower dentils. To give weight and balance to the room, the baseboard was marbleized.

In the library, bookshelves originally framed

A Regency-style mahogany drum table with drawers sits by the windows in the library. The Chippendale carved mahogany armchair with bowknot motif on the back was made in England, circa 1780. Bookcases on either side of the fireplace have been stripped to the natural wood. Between the windows, which are draped with fringed swags of rusty red damask backed with green, is a mid-nineteenth-century portrait of two children by Joseph Goodhue Chandler.

In the hall a mid-nineteenth-century American tall case clock has figures depicting the four seasons on its face. A Federal gilt wood-and-gesso girandole mirror, circa 1810–25, hangs above a centennial reproduction of a Hepplewhite table. In the living room beyond, sofa and easy chairs are covered in Brunschwig & Fils chintz. The carpet is a Mahal, circa 1900.

A dressing/sitting room is a private retreat for the woman of the house. Unashamedly feminine, the room is decorated with Scalamandré rose-covered chintz caught up in swags and rosettes on curtains by Robert Hollrotter of Fabriwerk; undercurtains are of festooned lace. A tiny geometric pattern is used for the skirted, kidney-shaped dressing table, while the seat in front gets a lace cover.

either side of the fireplace. Another wall of bookshelves was added and the surrounding radiator covers and baseboards were painted in matching faux bois. Uprights at the fronts of the bookcases were given carved details. This much-used room is the recipient of two noteworthy nineteenth-century portraits from the family farm. Books on painting, the decorative arts, and architecture are much in evidence, for the couple are avid students and collectors in these areas. To feather their Candela nest, they scouted the auctions and antique shops for furniture—much of it American antiques—and

while searching they became aware of American nineteenth-century paintings. They have been very careful to make sure that each piece in a room works well with all the other pieces. For this reason, the lawyer's large weight-lifting trophies (he is a former national weight-lifting champion) are kept hidden in a closet.

To assemble both paintings and furniture, the couple turned to Boston decorator Nancy Eddy, who gave valuable advice on fabrics, paint colors, and specialist craftsmen. The apartment reflects this highly traditional couple's polite and proper taste.

The Chinese wallpaper and the chandelier were inherited from the previous tenant. The 1660 painting *Peacocks and Other Birds in a Land-scape,* by Dutchman Melchior d'Hondecoeter, was on the cover of a Christie's auction catalog. On the table is Royal Crown Derby. The shield-back George III chairs are decorated with Prince of Wales feathers.

HAUTE BOHEME BED-SITTER

I n the area between lower Murray Hill (34th Street) and the upper Flatiron District (23rd Street), there are some buildings that started life as showrooms for the fur business. One, on Fifth Avenue, was turned into co-op apartments at the end of the 1970s. Conveniently close to midtown, the building is now filled with stylish people who prefer ample space to a smart address. The first to move in was Maxime de La Falaise. With English understatement she likes to point out that what she *really* lives in is a "large bed-sitter."

Maxime de La Falaise is one in a succession of famous beauties. Her mother, Lady Birley, was endlessly discussed not only for her beauty but for her daring style. Maxime followed this tradition both in her fashion designs and in the unforgettable images she created modeling couture clothes for the glossies in the 1940s and 1950s. Her daughter, Loulou, graduated from being one of the most photographed trendsetters of the sixties to being the well-organized muse of Yves Saint Laurent, for whom she designs costume jewelry and accessories, and the wife of Thadée Klossowski. Maxime's son, Alexis, as handsome as the women are lovely (it's the cheekbones!), is a furniture designer. His daughter, Lucie, has already appeared on a magazine cover, and Loulou's daughter, Anna, though only five, looks as if she will be making her photographic debut any minute. The whole family has an unmistakable larger-than-life chic, shunning the mundane for luxurious caravansaries.

Though Maxime has lived the latter part of her life in New York, she spent half of the earlier part in England and half in France. After the war she married Comte Alain de La Falaise, the father of her children. During her years in Paris she wrote and

styled for a fashion magazine, designed baby clothes for Schiaparelli, and was responsible for virtually "everything" in the Paquin boutique. In England she styled gloves for W. Pinkham & Son and shoes for Rayne. When she came to New York in the 1960s she had her own label, Blousecraft. Her second marriage, all too brief, was to John Mc-Kendry, curator of prints and photographs at the Metropolitan Museum. Since his death, Maxime has chosen to live in Manhattan lofts.

She found her bed-sitter loft through a tiny tease ad in the *New York Times*. Being an early tenant she was able to pick a high floor with fairly unimpeded views: a church, trees, Art Deco office roofs, studio windows, and small terraces that remind her of Montparnasse. In fact, the loft had too many windows. In her bedroom she gave up two of them to closet space; in the living room she installed new windows, blocking off others to make room for bookcases. Unhappy with the loft's thin walls, she had them thickened with plasterboard, creating deep window surrounds that were then mirrored. The thicker walls also disguised unsightly radiators and furnished the necessary depth for bookshelves. A nice detail on these shelves is a rounded wooden edge that gives them a substantial, finished appearance. When she moved in, the concrete living room floor was lower than the golden maple floor covering the rest of the space. To raise it, Maxime laid large terra-cotta tiles, bought raw from Country Floors. On this store's excellent advice, she herself finished the tiles in the classic way of Provence, a lengthy business involving linseed oil, turpentine, beeswax, acid, and much elbow grease.

Maxime devised a simple layout for the 2,350 square feet she had acquired, consulting an architect

Inspired by French surrealist writer Alfred Jarry, Maxime describes her steel four-poster—made for French Country Furniture by a blacksmith— as a "boat that moves only on land and whose sails are made of ancient Afghanistan embroidered hangings."

merely to draw up official plans. The space was divided into a living room and, catty-corner to it, a powder room for guests, and an open-plan kitchen with a scullery. Meals for up to six are served on a faux-painted round table in the living room, but for larger numbers there is a dining room, entered through engraved glass doors that can also be used to keep Maxime's three charmingly energetic dogs at bay. A long passage leads to the bedroom area. Next to it is the bathroom with its long walk-in closet, complete with utilities and a storage attic.

Maxime moved here from a loft ten blocks downtown. Her furniture was rolled up the street, piled on top of the building's elevator, and unloaded on her floor. The larger pieces, she remarks, are likely to be here forever because the building has since acquired new inner walls. Once installed, some of her possessions looked too rustic for this showroom-style building, so she had to urbanize her décor somewhat. Having neither terrace nor garden, she did, however, crave some boscage. The

ceiling was painted an unusual bright fondant green. English artist Graham Smith was asked to draw trees on the walls. Maxime requested silhouettes of similar tree shapes to form a pelmet over her living room window. By chance, a valance of Gothic-style gros point, picked up at a Parisian flea market and stored away for the future, fit the window perfectly. This kind of happenstance is the touchstone of the apartment, seen in the masterly way Maxime thrusts wildflowers into a vase or pulls together an impromptu but delicious meal.

Serious cooking is a major interest. Author of *The Seven Centuries Cookbook* (and now at work on an autobiographical culinary book), Maxime is known for her sumptuous feasts. She holds cooking classes in her loft and once, during a class devoted to making bouillabaisse, her favorite dog, Patch, of indeterminate breed, gave birth to six puppies under her bed. The whole class toasted each new arrival with white wine. Baby-Butts and Cokey, her other dogs, are Patch's puppies. Maxime uses a profes-

Carved of two kinds of wood, and furnished with massive hardware locks, an overscaled armoire found at a Manhattan downtown gallery marks the passage to the bedroom.

sional Garland stove ("they're built like Rolls-Royces"), though she turned in her ten-burner for a six-burner plus salamander. Persian tiles decorate the countertop. The scullery, tucked away behind a curtain, has a sink deep enough to hide dishes until after guests have gone. Pegged onto the kitchen counter is a series of barnyard-animal-shaped chopping boards—early designs by Alexis.

On the entrance door and exterior of the counter, pressed-metal ceiling squares have been used, a decorative and practical way of making them dogproof. Opposite the counter is a cedar closet that doubles as a room divider. A Graham Smith drawing of the Empire State Building is affixed to the end of this closet. Both closet and powder room doors are decorated with ruched curtains and borders—Maxime's decorative signature—using a mélange of vividly patterned fabrics found in the Middle East.

In the living room, sofas are covered with cherry-and-flower chintz found at the Marché Saint-Pierre at the foot of the Sacré-Coeur—a place where Maxime often bought fabric when designing her own collection in Paris. A slate-topped coffee table of diagonally cut wood matches the kitchen counters. Also in this room is a maquette of one of Alexis's tabletops, formed of different colored wood blocks that may be changed at will. Particularly vibrant are custom-made lamp shades of Yves Saint Laurent posters by Abat-jours Raspail. Dominating every-

Known for her cooking classes, recipe books, and brilliant little dinners, Maxime uses a professional, six-burner Garland stove with a salamander. A curtained scullery behind is fitted with a sink found on the Bowery.

In the living room hangs a portrait of Maxime's mother painted by her father, Sir Oswald Birley. The pelmet of silhouetted trees is by Graham Smith; the Gothic-style gros point below, found thirty years ago in the Marché aux Puces has finally been put to use. Centered on the windowsill is a nineteenth-century Japanese sake vessel. Kenzo bed pillows flank an Eastern saddlebag on the slipcovered sofa. The lamp shades are made from Yves Saint Laurent posters.

thing is a ravishing painting of Lady Birley painted by her husband, Sir Oswald Birley, a famous society and royal portrait painter, who was knighted for his services to the Crown.

The dining room has a round, faux-marble-topped table that supports a tall bronze doré-and-gilt candelabra. In a pinch, twelve can be seated around it on small French country chairs. A passage leading from dining area to bedroom is lined with furniture of varying origins, including a pair of outrageous tufted, divided-back Louis Philippe chairs bought in a mad moment.

In the bedroom, wall cupboards are fronted with natural wood lattice, backed with shirred fabric, and set in antiqued frames; the handles are unpolished brass window lifts. Antique embroidered hangings from Afghanistan enclose the tent-shaped four-poster. Piled with pillows, it has the exotic, thrown-together allure of a Bedouin camp, a deliberately antidecorated look.

The bathroom is an Aladdin's cave, with cupboards, shelves, and bowls dripping bijoux, many of them designed by Loulou. The walls are partly mirrored and partly upholstered with Indian bedspreads to which brooches can be pinned. The tall bathtub exterior is tiled in terra-cotta with jade green accents.

Much of the furniture has been bought at auction, and every piece tells a story. There is a chest whittled into faces and figures by Breton fishermen. Near it is a flea market vase crawling with porcelain lizards. Bunches of Venetian glass flowers are everywhere. These were bought almost sight unseen when Maxime glimpsed a few lilies of

the valley sticking out of a box in a sale. Remembering that they were her grandmother's favorite flowers, she snapped them up, only to discover masses more, including apple blossom and violets. Though there are times when Maxime insists she feels rootless living in the cement canyons of New York, her family's artistic roots run deep. The high bohemian effect is sumptuous without ever being pretentious, a mixture of styles and nationalities stirred up by a sophisticated chef.

MAYFAIR IN MANHATTAN

Until the 1920s, Sutton Place—which is technically a street, not a place—was predominantly industrial, filled with factories, a slaughterhouse, and a dirty coal yard. The name, which was adopted when the neighborhood began to get fancy, honors New York speculator Effingham Sutton, who, with his partner, John Phelps Stokes, first developed the area in 1875; before then, it was farmland belonging to one John Provost. Sutton himself lived near 57th Street in the end house of the street's first row of brownstones. In 1920 Anne Vanderbilt, widow of William K. Vanderbilt, rebuilt Sutton's house and persuaded her friends to follow her to this still unfashionable part of town. Anne Morgan, daughter of financier J. P. Morgan, moved next door, followed by America's first well-known decorator, Elsie de Wolfe, and her friend the theatrical agent and later politico Elisabeth (Bessie) Marbury. But it wasn't until the 1950s that Sutton Place became completely residential.

On the east side of the street, houses and apartment buildings look out onto gardens sharing a common lawn that extends to the bank of the East River. The view is unobstructed because the East River Drive (now the Franklin D. Roosevelt, or FDR, Drive) was built beneath the gardens. Now considered one of the most picturesque and secluded locations in the city, the area echoes the charm of London's Thames Embankment, but, because of the metallic 59th Street Bridge and view of an industrial area of Queens, it has a hard-edged New York mood. Perhaps its English overtones are what lured the present owners of a duplex to pick this pleasing location.

The seventeen-story building they chose to live in was completed in 1927. Designed by Man-

hattan's great luxury apartment-house architect Rosario Candela and constructed with the firm of Cross & Cross, the building can be compared with River House, a few blocks farther south; both buildings convey an image of affluent New York life. Candela's elegant triple-arched porte cochere opens onto a lobby that, in turn, opens onto the immaculately kept private garden overlooking the East River.

The owners, a newspaper publisher and writer, and his English wife, also a writer, raised their four children in a large apartment. With the children grown and no longer at home, the couple recently moved to a two-bedroom duplex in the Candela building on Sutton Place. For a year, they lived through the mayhem and discomfort of renovation ("We will *never* move again" says the wife), but now they are relieved that everything is as much in place as any intelligent residence should be.

Though Francophiles in most matters of taste, when it comes to decoration, the publisher and his wife are Anglophiles. At one time they had been advised by Tom Parr of the London-based firm of Colefax & Fowler. When he retired from active decorating, Parr suggested they consult Vivien Greenock, a young designer with Colefax & Fowler, for their Klosters house in Switzerland. The choice was a happy one. Lady Greenock's taste meshed so completely with her clients' that in the New York apartment it is difficult to tell which pieces of furniture came before or after Greenock. The duplex has been given the look of a cozy but smart cosmopolitan house in Mayfair. The legacy of John Fowler's décor (and Nancy Lancaster's—an American who influenced much of Fowler's work) looks at home here.

Perhaps the most discussed feature of the

The apartment overlooks the manicured lawn and shrubbery of the Candela building's private garden and, beyond it, the East River and Queens.

In a corner of the library, an unusual nineteenth-century Savonnerie carpet in soft greens lies upon the braided apple rush matting from Suffolk, England, that is used throughout the apartment.

On the library wall is a cherry painting by an anonymous Spanish contemporary artist. Over the fireplace is a mid-nineteenth-century French picture, embroidered with chenille, beads, metal, paper, and other media. The sofa is upholstered in a faux needlepoint linen. On it are antique needlepoint cushions and velvet cushions designed by George Oakes, depicting parrot tulips. To the right is a Regency cane-backed *bergère*. The chair in the foreground is upholstered in red mohair velour.

One corner of the drawing room features an eighteenth-century Dutch painted leather screen. The armchair is covered in Bailey Rose chintz and sits on a Bessarabian carpet.

duplex is the floor covering. Braided apple rush from Suffolk in England was selected and installed throughout. A neatly plaited rush edging borders this natural, wall-to-wall floor covering. Nowhere near as practical as traditional carpeting, it nevertheless gives a rustic charm to the apartment's traditional or more formal furniture. And it feels wonderful underfoot. The clients were forewarned that to prevent the rush from drying out and cracking it would have to be sprayed regularly like a garden. This watering makes it smell deliciously bucolic, like new-mown hay.

The owners were lucky because the apartment had previously belonged to only two other families and it was basically in good shape. The prior owners had gone totally modern, stripping out most of the ceiling moldings. Part of Vivien Greenock's brief, besides restoring these architectural embellishments—which were needed as background for the traditional English décor—was to help the traffic pattern of the apartment flow more easily. To accomplish this, doors were broken through in places and a fireplace closed off. In addition, a new staircase was built leading to the bedroom floor.

A small elevator hall leads into the oak-paneled library. Dark paneling was fashionable in Candela's day and many Americans liked to emulate the rarefied few who imported whole rooms of eighteenth-century paneling. Nowadays a more casual effect is in vogue and the wood in the library has been "limed" (sanded, stripped, and polished) to give it a lighter look. Faux marble paint work surrounds the fireplace. Next to a comfortable sofa, a bamboo side table with shelves and telephone becomes an informal desk for the lady of the house, who writes articles on ecological subjects and whose book, *Trees: An Anthology*, was published in 1989.

One of the newly added doors leads from library to drawing room. Both rooms look out over the communal greensward and the East River. Because the morning sun streams in, blinds of *very* English holland (a stiffened linen) and real London curtains (and no one makes these swagged, lined, interlined, braid-edged, and bullion-fringed numbers better than Colefax & Fowler) soften the glare. A Bessarabian rug and a pretty English needlepoint carpet complement the area of the drawing room where they are placed on top of the rush matting. Table and standing lamps have handmade shades of pleated and ruffled cream shantung. Cream beeswax candles adorn candelabra. Striped-silk-upholstered walls are embellished with a mix of beautifully framed and French-matted botanical prints, a George Oakes geranium painting, Italian architectural drawings, a painting on glass, and landscapes by Teddy Millington-Drake. Almost all the furniture comes from London, including several pieces from the shop started by the late English decorator Geoffrey Bennison. Sofas are loaded with antique needlepoint or painted velvet cushions collected

In the corridor off the drawing room, two salt-glaze King Charles spaniels sit on a marble-topped Irish table in front of a mirror edged in blue glass. Reflected in the mirror is an obelisk bookcase—a copy of Nancy Lancaster's in Charles Street, London—and pure Mayfair curtains of vivid pink taffeta.

An oak-and-elm William IV breakfast table is used for intimate meals in the dining room but can be enlarged with a cover to seat ten. For dinner parties, the room is lit by candles, including those on the tole chandelier. Fuchsia chintz covers walls and disguises cupboards containing flatware and china. The carpet is a rose-patterned Aubusson.

Peach pink with white dots Pheasant's Eye lines the walls of the master bedroom. The large reproduction bed from Colefax & Fowler is draped in Brompton Stocks chintz lined with Thistle voile. Bed and window curtains have two-color, linen fan edging. On the bed are beautifully laundered linens: some from Porthault, some embroidered-edged pillows with satin ribbon trim, and a white-on-white windowpane-checked quilt. Carpet is pale green flecked with white. A gros point overrug depicts a King Charles spaniel.

over the years on trips to London.

The walls of the corridor outside the drawing room are upholstered in a yellow minipatterned woven fabric. Beyond the drawing room the corridor has glazed walls of a similar color. The dining room off the corridor is small, but it can seat up to ten people when a cover is placed over the burlwood breakfast table. Fuchsia-patterned chintz walls conceal cupboards holding flatware, dinner sets, and glasses. Framed Indian prints decorate the walls. Beyond the dining room are a butler's pantry and kitchen. Both have been kept as originally designed by Candela but updated with new stove, refrigerator, and granite-topped counters.

The corridor terminates in the new, ingeniously engineered staircase that leads down to the bedroom floor. The staircase walls are studded with paintings by Teddy Millington-Drake and Derek Hill. The long corridor on this floor is lined with linen and clothing closets. Off of it is a guest suite, which is decorated in a white rose and aqua blue chintz from Colefax called Bowood. Also off the corridor is a powder room, a larger bathroom/dressing room for the man of the house, and at the end of the corridor, the master bedroom and its luxurious bathroom.

In the master bedroom the Colefax & Fowler reproduction canopied double bed is unusually high. The owner says it really belongs in a stately English home, but here it has the happy consequence of

being exactly the right height for one to lie in and gaze out the window at the garden and river. All the beds are beautifully curtained in the elegant Colefax & Fowler manner. This means hangings are interlined and lined with a contrasting fabric. Snap-in flower-sprigged linings can be laundered separately. Window curtains on this floor get the full C & F treatment, including undercurtains with a series of deep tucks at the bottom to finish them off. The walls are skillfully upholstered in the master bedroom so that seams line up with built-in closets. A screen composed of vintage prints and cut paper in one corner came from Sybil Connolly. An accumulation of pretty paper-covered boxes holds memorabilia. Braid and passementerie trim corners, door, and window frames. Chintz-covered armchairs are given nice touches such as a deep side pocket to hold magazines or needlework. Most inviting of all are the freshly pressed, flounced, lace-edged pillowcases on enormous pillows that fill half the bed.

Other touches are towel warmers in all bathrooms, heavy lace edges on thick white towels, luggage racks done up in Colefax & Fowler's seaweed-patterned chintz, and everywhere bowls of decoratively arranged potpourri studded with rosebuds. The impressive quality of the workmanship is echoed by impeccable housekeeping. The apartment, though luxurious, gives the impression of casual ease rather than opulence.

PERFECT SETTING ON GRAMERCY PARK

Gramercy Park, a historic district bounded by Lexington Avenue on the west and Third Avenue on the east and extending from 18th to 22nd streets, still possesses "tree-lined restraint," as architectural critic Paul Goldberger put it in *New York: The City Observed*. Though the fenced-in park itself is private and restricted to tenants who live in the surrounding buildings, the neighborhood has the appealing intimacy and limited traffic of a London square. Its eclectic houses, however, are strictly American. They include 1846 Andrew Jackson Davis brick houses with ironwork decorations, a church by James Renwick, Jr., an 1884 Gothic Revival brownstone by Calvert Vaux (of Olmsted & Vaux), and an 1888 Stanford White house built for actor Edwin Booth. In the 1920s building boom, large apartment houses were erected on the north side of the square, but otherwise there have been few changes since the nineteenth century.

The area's history dates back to 1651 when Peter Stuyvesant bought from the Dutch West India Company a farm consisting of a large tract of land, a house, barns, woods, six cows, two horses, and two young Negroes. According to Stephen Garmey's *Gramercy Park*, the property extended from what is today 3rd Street to 30th Street, and from the East River to 4th Avenue and Broadway. The name *Gramercy* derives in a rather roundabout way from a rise on this piece of land that the Dutch called *Krom Messje* (a corruption of "crooked swamp"), which by William III's time had become Crommessie. This was eventually simplified to Gramercy—though some people believe it derives from the French *grand merci*.

In the early days of European settlement, Indians still occupied much of the salt marshes and dense woods of this part of Manhattan. Part of this area was deeded by Peter Stuyvesant's widow, Judith, to a freed black slave, Francisco Bastiaense—a fairly common way to sustain a barrier between white settlers and Indians. It reverted back to the Stuyvesants after Bastiaense's death, and was sold to a member of a once-influential New York family, James De Lancey. (Only shabby Delancey Street remains to commemorate them.) He in turn sold it to his brother-in-law John Watts, who developed Love Lane, as the land just to the north of 21st Street was called in the eighteenth century. Watts then sold the area to another illustrious New Yorker, James Duane, who became the city's first mayor after the Revolution. In 1763 Duane bought more land from Watts in order to build what he called Gramercy Seat, a rural estate north of the early city. Its major houses were occupied by the British during the Revolution but Duane was fortunate in that his property was well cared for.

The man most responsible for the park as we know it today was developer Barclay Ruggles. He was born in 1800 in New Milford, then lived in Poughkeepsie. By the time he became a New York City developer, Manhattan had been laid out in the grid system, to the consternation of many citizens, who objected to the lack of green spaces within the scheme. Around the Gramercy Park area the grid was complicated because of undulating land. Chief landowner by then, Ruggles heeded traffic patterns and was sympathetic to the desire for green spaces. The development of Gramercy Park was his main—and no small—achievement. Its boundary followed the erstwhile Love Lane. Ruggles restricted the building around the park to residences, staunchly

forbidding the construction of foundries, breweries, or even theaters.

Ruggles appointed trustees to oversee the area. In 1832 they enclosed the park with iron railings. Plantsman William Laird selected fifty different shrubs and trees and James Virtue was employed as the park's first gardener. Ornamental walks were laid out in 1844. A fountain in the shape of a water nymph was placed in the center, later to be moved to one side of the park.

The first house facing the park was built in 1843. Other private residences went up as the century progressed. Since the 1860s many illustrious people have lived around Gramercy Park, including Governor Samuel J. Tilden, Stuyvesant Fish, James Harper, Edith Wharton, and, more recently, public

relations man Ben Sonnenberg.

Small though it is, nowadays Gramercy is a national park with a ranger on duty. A passerby, annoyed at not being able to get in, was told that the park is the "backyard" of the owners of the houses and apartments that surround it. The park is open to the public two days a year; otherwise one requires a key to enter. Keys are manufactured in Washington and changed periodically.

One of the apartment buildings on the north side of the park was begun in 1929. Because it was under construction when the crash came, fireplaces drawn on the plans were never completed, though many apartments in the building still have non-functioning mantels. Designer Peri Wolfman, a Parsons graduate, and photographer Charles Gold—

In the living room, off-white arm-less sofas are draped in dazzling white antique Marseilles spreads, crocheted covers, or quilts. A collection of white ceramic pigs and jugs sits on the coffee table of untreated wood made from a brick pallet. This white-on-white room is offset by a natural pine French Provincial armoire. The teddy bear next to it is of white-on-white jacquard cotton. On the other side of it is a stepped screen designed by Charles Gold. The terrace overlooks Gramercy Park.

owners of Wolfman-Gold & Good Company—moved in around 1980. Their shop in a SoHo landmark building specializes in heavy white restaurant pottery, plain pine furniture, wicker, and white household fabrics. Peri Wolfman, who used to design children's clothes on Seventh Avenue and now has turned to interior design, is mainly responsible for the strong personal flavor of both shop and apartment. She spent some years in California and acquired a taste for fresh, uncluttered surroundings and a need for nearby greenery. The apartment, with its terrace overlooking the park, satisfied these requirements. Both Wolfman and Gold lead busy lives, so their rule is to pare down and simplify. They agreed to stick to white as their basic decorating color and to use natural wood textures to offset it.

The apartment was modernized in the late 1950s or early 1960s. On one ceiling they found a reproduction of a Mondrian painting in fluorescent lights. Though it may have been madly fashionable when installed—it was featured in a 1960s decorating magazine—it was the first thing to be ripped out. To keep the apartment sleek and modern, picture rail moldings were removed. Walls were painted white. In several places, different levels were incorporated into the design of the rooms to break up the space. In the living room, for instance, a step leading up to the terrace overlooking the park was extended to stretch all across that side of the room. In the dining room, a platform was installed under the lace-curtained window to accommodate a cushioned wicker sofa. Concealed lighting was introduced in the foyer and track lighting elsewhere.

In the foyer, which is given some scale by huge stone vases filled with amusing combinations of flowers such as formal white gladiolus and modest September weed, the floor-to-ceiling shelves are filled with Charlie Gold's display of antique cameras, hand-colored photographs, and daguerreotypes and cases, all collected since the late 1960s from thrift shops.

A wood ceiling fan cools the master bedroom. On the bed is a white crocheted coverlet and hemstitched, lace-edged, tatted-edged, damask-woven, and buttoned pillows. Clothes are kept in a plain pine wardrobe and a highly organized walk-in closet. In the storage unit behind the bed, shelves hold books and oddments.

As Gold is also a chef manqué, a professional kitchen was a prerequisite. It involved major renovation of the existing kitchen, including stealing space from what had been maids' rooms. Part of this area is now a utilities room—and the place where the family's cats can hide from the two dogs. The present kitchen is based on an open plan. A bar divides the cooking area from the dining room, where there was once a wall with a door. It opens up a long vista through the foyer to the living room, giving a clear view of daylight from one side of the apartment to the other.

If Charlie is the cook, Peri is the one who sets the table. Her ideas on this subject are so strong they have filled one book already. *The Perfect Setting* was conceived by the couple and features his photographs of her decorative tables.

Lest one get the impression that this is a yuppie couple living a pampered, selfish life, one must realize that they have plenty of domestic responsibilities. With a combined family of four teenage boys, the way of life must be simple and practical. Beds in one of the boys' rooms have been placed on different stepped levels. In another, the beds are bounded by low shelves. The effect is spartan, minimal, and somewhat *japonais*, aided by the gray carpeting, black-and-white-print sheets, and gener-

To simplify the décor, household crockery has been pared down to all white, mostly thick, restaurant-type pottery and the simple restaurant glasses and pitchers seen here above the double sink.

Converted from the old kitchen and pantry, this chef's dream of a kitchen is Charlie Gold's domain. The restaurant-sized Wolf double stove includes a grill, griddle plate, and sturdy gas burners. Counter space is topped with crude white tiles or butcher block. Precisely organized shelves and drawers contain cook's tools. Leaded casement windows provide plenty of light.

The unfinished pine dining room table is surrounded by white-painted, armless Windsor chairs. A billiard table light fixture hangs overhead. The antique carved-wood Irish mirror was stripped of its gilding. Paper doilies echo the Chinese lace curtains from Wolfman-Gold & Good Company. Oval restaurant plates hold white embroidered napkins and are flanked by white-handled knives and forks.

ally Comme des Garçons colors.

Peri Wolfman, Charles Gold, and their brood are living proof that the life-style they sell in their shop really works. They love the purity of white, as exemplified in the stacks of white towels and plain white shower curtain in the bathroom, a place where even Peri's silvery steel necklaces look decorative hanging on brass hooks. In closets, clothes are kept to a minimum but are beautifully hung on matching,

practical hangers. Wicker baskets and chests hold quilts and coverlets. Varieties of flatware, some ornate, some naive, fill drawers. Collections of napkins include humble cotton bandannas and unusual dishcloths. Pottery—chosen for its weighty, sculptural quality—and oversize glasses fill the cupboards. Everything is used, and near to hand. And ideas, simple and affordable, are always percolating to create the perfect setting.

VILLAGE TRADITIONAL

Judith Schneider was born in Mount Vernon, New York. While attending Sarah Lawrence College she met Leah Lenney, who, many years later, was to become the interior designer for her New York apartment. After living in Los Angeles and Boston, Dr. Schneider, a psychologist, returned to New York and rented an apartment in a Greenwich Village town house. A few years later she bought the building and began to renovate the ground-floor apartment, shortly after marrying lawyer-businessman Norbert Weissberg.

Until settling in New York, Judith Schneider had always lived in houses, thus amassing a fair amount of furniture. She wanted a place where she could use it, and also walk out into a garden. The house in Greenwich Village with its Greek Revival elegance fit the bill.

The house was built in 1837–38, during the surge in tract-house construction developed by the Astor family. In the 1830s and 1840s entire blocks were produced for the city as it rapidly grew northward. This area of Greenwich Village—by then no longer a village but a town—was established around Grace Church at 11th Street and Broadway. From the beginning this Gothic Revival church—designed by the young architect James Renwick, who at the time had yet to see a genuine Gothic building—was a fashionable place of worship. Though some imposing residences were built in the area for the affluent, many of the row houses were erected without any specific owner in mind. They were as speculative as anything built today, though most current developers seem to have lost the knack of creating dwellings as good-looking or long-lasting as these.

The houses surrounding Dr. Schneider's have the same basic plan, with a kitchen at the back and dining room at the front, both on the ground floor. The parlor floor, entered from outside by walking up a short flight of steps, consisted of two parlors divided by a sliding door. A restored version of these houses is the Old Merchant's House on East 4th Street. Changing needs, social patterns, and lack of room to expand have altered the original uses of various rooms, and today the interiors of most of these houses have been greatly modified, though the attractive exteriors have fortunately been left intact.

The builder was I. Greene Peason. Dr. Schneider's apartment still boasts its original wrought-iron area railings and floor-length parlor windows. When the house was built, the back garden would have included an outhouse and a place for laundry. The washing would have been hung out to dry, for the combination of sunlight and green grass produced sweet-smelling laundry, a luxury we have discarded in favor of the more convenient drying machine. The house remained a single-family dwelling until some seventeen years ago, when it was broken up into separate units. Renovations at that time included the addition of a kitchen wing all the way from ground level to the roof.

Dr. Schneider's renovations started in 1986. She consulted her architect son-in-law, James Simon, who admits it was a good test of familial relations. Jim had married Judith Schneider's daughter, Audrey, in the town house's garden before the renovations began, so he had a special interest in the place. To make the garden perfect for the celebration, garden designer Cory Davenport, who specializes in town-house gardens, was called in; he worked on it for several months before the wedding and arranged the flowers for the event.

The brick-paved garden, in luxurious bloom, makes an ideal setting for lunch.

In the renovated kitchen, marble counters are from Manhattan Marble Co., oven range and hood from Gaggenau, sink from Just Co., fittings from Chicago Faucet Co., refrigerator from Sub-Zero Refrigeration, lighting from Halo Halophane, and switching from Lutron. *(right)*

The center shelf of a pine dresser holds a collection of maple syrup jugs. Above and below is pottery from the twenties and thirties, and on the counter are two tin tobacco jars and family snapshots.

In the master bedroom, French windows lead out into the garden. An antique trunk below the oval mirror stores seat pads used for summer garden furniture. Brunschwig & Fils chintz covers the armchair, which holds a needlepoint cushion by Leah Lenney. Next to it an Edwardian bamboo table displays Japanese netsukes. A handmade afghan throw decorates the foot of the Ralph Lauren wicker bed.

Simon came up with the basic architectural plan for the project, keeping in mind the historical aesthetic of the building and its setting. The major decisions took a year. General goals included making over the kitchen—which involved gutting a small pantry, completely revamping the existing kitchen, and doubling storage space for less-used seasonal equipment. The space also yielded a small powder room now leading off the hall. The rest of the apartment required a lot of unobtrusive cabinetwork in storage areas, and the ground-floor bathrooms were completely remodeled. Luckily, many of the original interior details were still intact: shutters, crown moldings, pillars, window entablatures, and working fireplaces. Such details would have been selected from several available variations at the lumberyards, thus permitting these mid-nineteenth-century speculative houses some individuality within the general scheme. With preservation of these decorative elements in mind, Simon recommended a local specialist, Nick Tannone of Village Contracting Company, as general contractor.

Interior designer Leah Lenney became involved early on. Though architect and decorator are of different generations, their collaboration was unusually close, fused by the strong historical emphasis of the job. Lenney worked with Dr. Schneider, incorporating furniture she already owned, buying other pieces as needed, and selecting wall coverings, fabrics, and carpets. Schneider says that the interaction between them was a great learning process for her, while Lenney discovered that her client had a good eye, which she learned to trust.

During the year it took to complete the renovations, Schneider and Weissberg lived like nomads. Their predicament is not unusual in New York, where huge amounts of money have to be invested in a residence and little is left for alternate digs. The couple chose to live in and work around the chaos, and survived.

Both front and back parlors have been fitted with floor-to-ceiling bookshelves on their fireplace wall. Rolling ladders (from Putnam Rolling Ladder Company) make the books accessible. On some shelves, Weissberg's collections of antique Roman glass, Greco-Roman pottery, and other early artifacts have been arranged. The wood floors are new but have been carefully made to look like the originals by antiquarian I. M. Wiese of Southbury, Connecticut. Between the two original pillars dividing the parlors would have been slots for sliding mahogany doors but this space is now taken up by conduits bringing pipes to the upper floors. Part of the back parlor is used as a dining room, with the table

overlooking the back garden. The sideboard is the base of an enormous pine country dresser found in England—the original shelves reached up twenty feet but these were never brought to America—and an antique footbath has become a container for plants. Master and guest bedrooms, two bathrooms, and Weissberg's study are all downstairs on the garden floor.

The house doesn't scream out that it has just been "done" by architect or decorator, but gives the impression that it has been lived in for some time. This is due in part to the restraint of Simon and Lenney, and to the personal accumulations of the owners; it is the essence of what constitutes a home in the city.

The original back parlor is now a combination sitting room, library, and dining room. The sofa is covered in Brunschwig & Fils chintz called L'Arbre Exotique. The green antiqued dining room chairs came from Dr. Schneider's house in California. Prints of Roman vases are from Stephanie Hoppin.

MODERN CRAFTS

For some, New York City is home; for others, such as Southerners Edward and Susie Elson, it is the ideal place for a pied-à-terre. Edward Elliott Elson, founder of a chain of hotel and airport gift shops, and his wife, Susie, chairman of the American Crafts Council, made a decision about four years ago to sell their business and restructure their lives. They now maintain their base in Atlanta, spend one week every month in their London flat, one week traveling, and one week in their New York apartment. As a pied-à-terre it is quite grand—a duplex penthouse, complete with terraces, on Park Avenue.

Mrs. Elson was brought up in Memphis in a traditionally decorated house. At college in Virginia, she began to take an interest in contemporary crafts, partly as a rebellion against the antiques, chintz, and Oriental carpets of her home. Luckily, her husband's tastes coincided with hers, though he admits it is mostly Susie's choices that set the confrontational and witty tone of their New York apartment.

The space previously belonged to a movie mogul and exuded a distinctly fifties ambience. The Elsons brought in architect Irv Weiner from Atlanta, where he had remodeled their Tudor-style mansion. Whereas many New York apartments are shielded by blinds or heavy curtains to protect precious carpets and fragile works of art from the destructive effects of daylight, Weiner's major challenge was to bring light in, because he was making a setting for sturdy, functioning crafts. Light was particularly needed in the long, dark entrance hall. To accomplish this, he designed suave floor-to-ceiling windows set in gray frames with bronze hardware. Light now pours into the living room, master bedroom, and dressing room; interior walls of glass brick surrounding the dressing room carry diffused light through to the hall.

The penthouse came with a glass-roofed sun room—now called the porch—which let daylight in at one end of the hall. Mrs. Elson commissioned Narcissus Quagliata to design and execute a stained-glass window to replace the wall between the porch and the adjacent dining room. This glass wall not only brings light into the dining room during the day, but also works as a screen decorated in a geometric, abstract style.

In commissioning such inventive built-in architectural furnishings, Mrs. Elson worked closely with the artists as well as with architect Weiner. He created an ideal background. Floors of blond maple and gray-stained oak give a light and airy ambience. Clean white walls, recessed ceiling lights, built-in shelves of concrete, steel, or glass to hold collected objects are all part of this environment. The main reception rooms—living room, dining room, and porch—open off the hall without doors, giving an unimpeded flow to the layout. A well-composed banister of maple and white-painted metal borders the staircase that leads down to a guest suite with an independent entrance below. The kitchen complex—including laundry and ironing room, small terrace, maid's room, and large kitchen—is simple and practical. The selection of decorative fabrics was entrusted to English interior designer and writer Mary Gilliat, who had helped decorate the Elsons' London flat.

Every detail shows intelligence and a keen sense of quality. Much of this can be discerned only by actually touching the superb finish of surfaces of both the architectural background and the craft pieces. Even that New York essential—sturdy inside door locks—are chrome-finished. As an avid sup-

At the far end of the hall, bleached maple flooring changes to gray-stained oak with maple inlay. The metal hall table with inset optic lens and painted "eyes" resembling magnified ostrich skin is by André Debreuil. On it are a shagreen sphere and a Mattia Bonetti silver clock. Shelves hold ceramic pots by Svend Bayer.

porter of the crafts movement, Mrs. Elson commissioned most of the furnishings for this space. One exception is a red-and-silver lacquered screen by Art Deco craftsman Jean Dunand that was shown at the 1925 Paris *Exposition Internationale des Arts Décoratifs et Industriels Modernes.* It is displayed on the wall as a work of art rather than on the floor as a functioning screen. Its prominence in the hall is shared with paintings by Rainer Fetting, Philip Wofford, and Anselm Kiefer, as well as an unnerving but unforgettable Sandro Chia nude with stockings—the latter being Edward Elson's acquisition. Equally intriguing is Elizabeth Browning Jackson's rug, which zigzags in jagged points along the hall. Tailored to the space, and of great quality, it was obviously not designed by an ordinary commercial carpet manufacturer. Jackson also invented an irregularly shaped hall table that holds glass pieces by Harvey Littleton, an artist-craftsman whom Mrs. Elson trailed from London's Victoria and Albert

Museum to Wisconsin and back to London before being able to buy his art glass. Nearby is a textile hanging called *Corporate Sails,* by Gloria Crouse of Olympia, Washington. It is fashioned like the shaggy, handmade rag hearth rugs found in English cottages but composed of a sophisticated mix of businessmen's suiting—gray flannel, pinstripes, tweeds—and shirting, odd flashes of silver lamé, and grommeted industrial carpeting.

Branching off the hall to the right is the living room. Confronted by its grand piano, one cannot resist a smile. The instrument started life in late-nineteenth-century Dresden but was completely reconstructed as a piece of sculpture by Fred Baier. Each leg is a neo-Brancusiesque-via-Memphis work of art; every surface is coated with varied, unexpected hues of shiny automobile paint; even the inner workings are meticulously colored. It is still a functioning instrument, however, so one can only imagine a piano tuner's surprise! Equally wild and

Zigzagging along the hall is a carpet designed for the space by Elizabeth Browning Jackson. A maple-and-metal banister leads downstairs to the guest suite below, passing a wall hanging, *Corporate Sails,* by Gloria Crouse. Paintings include *New York Painter* (1983) by Rainer Fetting, *Little Warrior* (1981) by Philip Wofford, and at end of hall, *Unsinkable Framed Figure* (1982) by Sandro Chia.

A corner of the living room features Fred Baier's ardent folly—a sculptural, vividly painted grand piano. Behind it is a German neo-Expressionist painting, *Die Fahat II*, by Rainer Fetting. A chair of polished ebony with hands carved on the arms is by Bob Trotman.

Totally restored, painted in pink, black, purple, and turquoise car enamel, with even the interior soundboard, plate, and hitch pins dyed to match, the piano bears an inscription that reads: "Reconstructed in London, England by Fred Baier for the Elson Family, New York, 1989."

Porch furniture is overscale wicker from Wicker Works. A commissioned print on heavy raw silk by Sian Tucker covers the cushions. The blanket on the ottoman is by Hilary Auden. The trisectioned glass coffee table, bolted with oxidized metal and glass, is by Danny Lane. Ceramic pots sit on rough-sanded cement shelves, wall brackets, and thick glass shelves. On the right is Sandro Chia's *Unsinkable Framed Figure*. (preceding spread)

Glass-topped side table by Peter Pierobon has seven varied legs. The bed, of bleached maple with ebony inlay and silver-leafed touches, was commissioned from Edward Zucca. The cream woven fabric on the bed is from Clarence House. In the hall beyond can be seen a papier-mâché sculpture, *The Butler*, by Stephen Hansen.

entertaining is the fireplace, decorated with a face and hands by Scottish artist Bruce McLean. His black iron mantel slants so that it can accommodate both short and tall people. In the living room is another of Gloria Crouse's pieces, a rug made of strips of woven wool and bear fur interspersed with rows of metal washers and fringed with woolen pigtails. Comfortable upholstered furniture includes gray velvet-covered armchairs made in the 1930s and a sofa covered in textured leather, wrinkled to resemble elephant hide. Small pillows are scattered on these pieces; far from being predictable needle-point or fashionable carpet-covered cushions, they are decorated with squeezed-on rubber squiggles or made of velvet, screen-printed in gold. The room contains several chairs that are designed not for comfort but for their sculptural qualities. One combines polished brass, red-painted metal, and wire. Two others are of twisted wire. The most conventional thing in the room is a trio of African sculptures.

Next to the living room is the master bedroom with its accompanying bathroom, and a dressing room that Mrs. Elson uses, in the French tradition, as a *cabinet*, or private office. A curved dressing table, lit from above, serves as a desk. Next to it is a Mark Brazier-Jones purple-seated chair with wings of polished steel on a Mondrianesque bias-slanted,

textured, silver-shot rug, another of Gloria Crouse's works. For the master bedroom, Susie Elson commissioned Edward Zucca to invent an impressive four-poster in blond maple inlaid with ebony. A full moon of silvered gold is set on the center of the headboard and silvery tips terminate each of the four posts, like guardian saints. A simple geometric bedside rug by Elizabeth Eakins lies on the blond maple floor. More unexpected is the bedside table by Peter Pierobon, its seven twisted legs resembling chic Irish shillelaghs.

On the opposite side of the hall is the kitchen complex, dining room, and porch. A series of shelves in the dining room displays Mrs. Elson's collection of art glass. The table is another of Bruce McLean's inventions, a great circular expanse of polished terrazzo decorated with two faces. Part of the table's support is a hand. Surrounding it are stainless steel chairs commissioned from Tom Penn, son of photographer Irving Penn. As with all the commissioned furniture in the apartment, there were false starts: before these chairs were deemed totally comfortable there were as many as fifteen prototypes considered. They have gray suede seats and back pads—the latter on springs attached to the seat so that the back moves with the sitter. Opposite Quagliata's glass wall is a neo-German Expressionist painting by Jorg Immendorf. A cabinet beside the glass wall was made in Paris by Garouste and Bonetti.

The porch, true to its name, is appointed with live greenery and wicker furniture. In this room the wood flooring changes from the warm maple to a cooler gray-stained oak inlaid with maple. A wall displays ceramics by artists and craftsmen including Nancy Adams, Gordon Baldwin, Svend Bayer, Bennet Bean, a watermelon by Ned Cartledge, Ruth Duckworth, Peter Hayes, Ed and Philip Moulthrop, Magdelena Oqundo, Ed Rossback, and Harvey Sadow. Below the built-in shelves are a couple of small stools dressed in grass skirts, also by Garouste and Bonetti. A glass coffee table by Danny Lane looks positively lethal; it is made of what appears to be broken glass held together by rusty bolts. The glass, however, when touched, has a smooth finish. On the table is a moon-headed man riding a toylike horse, a woven silver basket, and an aluminum plate. Another table topped by a pink vinyl pie frill is by Tim Walker.

Beyond the porch the hall turns a corner and doors open out onto the terrace. Gray-painted stucco lines this part of the hall. More shelves and brackets display ceramic vases. For privacy a tiny desk with a telephone is tucked away in a niche, and nearby stands a tall-backed, painted-metal chair from a contemporary Japanese workshop.

The guest suite on the floor below is decorated somewhat more conventionally. Stairs lead down into a sitting room that can be closed off from the bedroom, dressing room, and bathroom by mahogany-paneled doors. Mahogany bookcases and a bar face the sitting room and serve as a room divider. Backing these bookcases are cupboards, including a wine cellar, that are part of a guest kitchen tucked under the stairs. Even here no detail is mundane. On the kitchen floor lies a grin-provoking, checkered bear-shaped rug by Pucci de Rossi. The sitting room is furnished with classic modern furniture: Le Corbusier's *Grand Confort* cube armchairs, upholstered in black leather and set on tubes of chromium-plated steel; a tubular chrome side table; a pony-skin-covered chaise longue; a sofa loaded with faux-animal-print cushions; and a coffee table of Macassar ebony designed by Martin Grierson. In keeping with the more traditional style of the suite, decorative objects include a 1790 Japanese lacquered box and an 1830 Japanese walking stick and shopping bag. Two dramatic graphite portraits by Alfred Leslie dominate one wall. The most riveting piece of furniture is a fabulously bizarre desk of blond burlwood and gilt, with accents of ebony and white marble. Though the chair beside it looks more decorative than utilitarian, this is the kind of desk that might inspire fantastic fairy tales.

Orchestrated by Susie Elson, this pied-à-terre is full of marvels. Its elements—modern, functional architecture; German Expressionist art; and superbly made crafts—all combine to make a cohesive, provocative and generally lighthearted symphony.

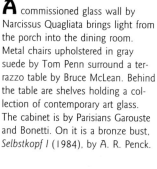

A commissioned glass wall by Narcissus Quagliata brings light from the porch into the dining room. Metal chairs upholstered in gray suede by Tom Penn surround a terrazzo table by Bruce McLean. Behind the table are shelves holding a collection of contemporary art glass. The cabinet is by Parisians Garouste and Bonetti. On it is a bronze bust, *Selbstkopf I* (1984), by A. R. Penck.

MURRAY HILL MAGNIFICENCE

Between the wide thoroughfares of 34th and 42nd streets, and east of Fifth Avenue to Lexington Avenue, rises the gentle slope of a Manhattan residential area known as Murray Hill. It was named after Robert Murray, who, during the Revolutionary period, owned a large estate surrounding his then-isolated mansion in the vicinity of what is now 37th Street and Park Avenue. At the southern end of Murray's estate was Kips Bay (now 34th Street), where British troops landed just two weeks after winning the Battle of Long Island in 1776. The Murrays played a pivotal part in the Revolutionary drama: Robert Murray's wife cannily served tea to British General William Howe and his military staff, no doubt piling on charm as well as victuals. She detained them long enough for the depleted American forces to escape north.

In the nineteenth century, as Manhattan's grid of streets and avenues spread northward, Murray Hill began to be developed, as Charles Lockwood describes in *Bricks and Brownstone:* "During the 1860s, mansions and elegant brownstone-fronts were built along Fifth, Madison, and Park avenues and 34th Street, and fine row houses filled Lexington Avenue and the side streets from Sixth to Third avenues." *New York Times* architectural critic Paul Goldberger states: "There is an elegance to Park Avenue here, more understated than elsewhere, but real. . . . Even the apartment houses here choose not to shout, as so many of their uptown brethren do."

Murray Hill had become a fashionable neighborhood by 1898, when a dignified but stylish brown brick-and-brownstone Italian Renaissance "palazzo" was built at Park Avenue and 35th Street for J. Hampton Robb by McKim, Mead & White.

The building later became the Advertising Club. In the late 1970s the club was converted into cooperative apartments.

The first to move in was costume jewelry designer Kenneth Jay Lane, who acquired the *piano nobile,* with its balcony facing the street, and the front apartment on the floor above. Because he was involved in the building's renovation from the start, Lane was able to plan the space as he wished. No stranger to the visual arts—he used an architect only for technicalities—Lane incorporated into his design many of the splendid features of the original building. In his high-ceilinged entrance hall, formerly the building's stairwell, he has installed a staircase that ascends to a book gallery, then turns and proceeds up to the bedroom floor. The originally planned three bedrooms were revamped into a master bedroom adjoining a palatial bathroom, and a guest room.

The original renovation plan for the *piano nobile* included a large dining room and small kitchen. Lane opted instead for a small dining area, bounded by a screen, to the right of the stairs. The kitchen, presided over by Lane's French majordomo, Raymond, is tucked in a corner to the right of the entrance. Intimate dinners for eight or nine can be shoehorned into the dining area. For larger numbers—as many as sixty can be entertained—a buffet is served and guests mingle in the front reception room. The splendor of this great room has been left intact. The elaborate molded plaster ceiling remains, though in the days of the Advertising Club it was painted a dirty brownish gold. Two rather-too-grand entrances opened into the original room. One set of double doors led to the next apartment, so Lane filled it in with bookcases. He gave the other entrance

A fantasy chair made of horns sits beside a table holding Indian metal animals. The camel is Persian. The William Acton drawing of Diana Vreeland is a preliminary sketch for the jacket of her book *D.V.* The ivory column beside it is about to be made into a lamp base. Tucked among the books on the shelves are pieces of Chinese jade.

a smaller door and then surrounded it with more bookcases. Now crammed with volumes, especially on architecture and the decorative arts, these bookcases look as if they have always been there. The opulent marble fireplace remains, ornamented with impressive *objets de vertu.*

Kenneth Jay Lane was born in Detroit and studied at the University of Michigan and the Rhode Island School of Design. His work in the art department at *Vogue* and then as a shoe designer for Delman and Christian Dior eventually led him to jewelry design. Since 1963 his name has been at the forefront of fashion. The prestigious Coty American Fashion Critics Special Award for "Outstanding Contribution to Fashion" and awards from Neiman-Marcus, *Harper's Bazaar,* and Tobé Coburn are only some of his citations. Frequently on the International Best-Dressed Men's list, Lane is an urbane, elegant spokesman of style. A glance at his stack of invitations shows he is in demand at New York's smartest gatherings, where he is a witty and suave escort to New York's most glamorous women.

For his bedroom, Lane—who has long been fascinated by classical architecture—designed an elaborate fireplace, mantel, and wall of clothes cupboards that involved twenty ebonized and bronze-doré columns. Though it "took forever!" the results are worth the effort. Inspired by the library of the British Embassy in Paris as it was decorated by Georges Geoffroy for the Duff Coopers just after World War II, Lane fronted the cupboard doors with chicken wire mesh. Similar wire mesh is also used on the bedroom door. His bathroom suite, a masculine combination of dark green marble and light wood, might be every gent's dream.

Though not a professional decorator, Lane is aware that before the first piece of furniture enters a room, the background—paint finish, floors, and curtains—must be absolutely right. In this most crucial and complex aspect of *le haut décor* he has excelled. The faux paint work is impeccable. Whether the walls are upholstered or painted, the curtains simple or elaborate, they enhance each room without taking over. For instance, the tall windows in the living room are festooned with heavy Roman-striped cotton. The fabric is not overly expensive, but the curtains look luxurious because they are copied exactly from ones made under the direction of

In this hall, which also serves as the dining room, the stairway installed by Lane leads to a book gallery, then to the bedroom floor. The table is set with nineteenth-century Bohemian overlay glass wine decanters and Venetian cranberry glass goblets. The lamp base is American Empire. On the red-lacquered wall is a portrait of Lane and some Luigi Meyer architectural drawings. The paneled doors are Russian burl.

71

A large and luxurious bathroom with shower and dressing room is lined with verd antique marble and light-colored wood painted by Malcolm Robson to look like burl. *(right)*

Lane's bedroom serves as a part-time office, hence the cluttered table. Elaborate architectural details around the fireplace include ebonized columns with gilt-bronze capitals supporting a central pediment. In front of the mottled overmantel mirror is a Hellenistic torso. Passementerie braid borders the wide green satin striped wall covering, which is also used for the outer bed curtains. The fabric was specially made by Lowenstein. The inner curtains are of striped cotton from Schumacher.

London's high priest of decoration, John Fowler. Lane had to show his upholsterer how to avoid the usual temptation of making the curtains too exaggeratedly ballooned.

Before settling in the J. Hampton Robb house, Lane had accumulated many treasures, but like any true collector, he is constantly amassing more. A sophisticated and frequent traveler—he visits India at least once a year—he always returns with treasures found off the beaten path, such as one-of-a-kind woven dishcloths used to cover cushions, or silk saris to upholster an ottoman. He likes to point out chairs that he bought for pennies in a Palermo flea market and then somewhat ruefully describe how a fortune was spent transporting them back to New York and getting them upholstered.

A wealth of furniture fills the space; at last count, six sofas, three ottomans, and thirteen chairs of varying styles and sizes graced the living room. Nothing is static. A swatch of tartan draped over the back of a child's chair in the bedroom and piles of Indian gold-thread-and-silk fabrics stacked on a bench in the living room await the upholsterer. The cumulative effect, far from being haphazard, is supremely luxurious. It is difficult to believe that

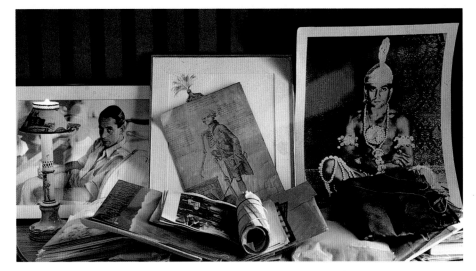

the sofas are covered not in expensive and fragile *gaufrage* but in far more mundane and practical Herculon, impervious to everything, says Lane, but cigarette ash, which makes it melt! Books, furniture, and objects have obviously been chosen with affection, and such loving abundance imparts relaxed informality to this magnificent mansion.

A side table in the bedroom is loaded with books, prints, packages, and photographs, including two of Lane himself.

A "Turkish corner" in the living room displays Orientalia. Pictures include work by Sir Lawrence Alma-Tadema, Benjamin-Constant, Edwin Weeks, David Roberts, and Adam Bell. A Korean table holds Indian shell and mother-of-pearl powder horns. Sofa cushions are made from Indian handwoven dishcloths picked up for seventy-five cents apiece.

Above the original marble fireplace is a George II mirror. On the mantel are seventeenth-century Italian marble busts of Mars and Athena. Terracotta slaves by Piero Tocca flank a bronze hermaphrodite. The easel holds a James Green picture of Indian jugglers, 1814. The cord-embellished foreground chairs, found in Palermo, are covered in Brunschwig & Fils velvet.

THIRTIES GRAPHICS

Not far from his workplace—the Reinhold Brown Gallery at 26 East 78th Street—Robert Brown owns a unique apartment. His gallery specializes in posters and the work of important graphic designers from all over the world, especially Europe. Appropriately, his apartment used to belong to Lucian Bernhard, a German designer famous in the early part of the century for his innovative posters, typography, and furniture design.

The apartment is in a building that was constructed in the early twenties. Recently the whole building was renovated and made over into cooperative apartments. The street entrance is now done up in slick, yuppie gray granite and steel finishes. The contrast on reaching the Brown apartment is vivid, a sixty-year step back in time. The hallway features an astonishing translucent ceiling, lit from above and decorated with black Art Deco triangles. A shiny black floor contrasts with outrageous flamingo pink walls. A hall table juts out from the wall, as do a built-in bench and wooden coat hooks. The place must have been startlingly modern in 1930 when Lucian Bernhard designed it.

Robert Brown heard about Lucian Bernhard's apartment from a colleague who worked at La Boetie, a gallery specializing in German paintings and posters. A Lucian Bernhard poster was once displayed in the window of this gallery when Bernhard himself happened to pass by. He entered the gallery, introduced himself, and soon he and the employee became friends. When Bernhard died, Brown went to see the apartment—which intrigued him—with a view to renting it. The place was a mess and hadn't been painted in years, but the original furniture—much of it built in—was all there. Brown was thrilled by the place and by the idea of living

in an apartment designed by Bernhard, whom he had long admired. He acquired it in mid-1972 and decided to retain the authentic look as an *hommage à* Bernhard. He got in touch with Bernhard's son, Karl, who was helpful in recalling the true colors of the paint work, carpets, and upholstery, much of which required repair or replacement. But he changed very little of Lucian Bernhard's original design.

Though not a big apartment by some East Side standards, it was used not only as a residence but also as a studio where a small coterie of commercial artists produced prototype brochures, catalogs, and advertisements under Bernhard's direction. Most of the designer's brilliant early poster work had been done in Germany prior to his emigration to America, but in the United States he composed many typefaces, some of which still bear his name. His original studio—now the living room—and office were lined with storage units of all sizes. Some of them, especially those in the living room, consist of low, flat drawers designed to hold extra-large sheets of paper. There are also vertical spaces for portfolios, and in the study is a wooden rack resembling an outsize magazine stand, designed as a place on which heavy portfolios could rest.

After Brown moved in, he was able to explore at leisure this complex of built-in cupboards that Bernhard had shoehorned into the space—a veritable essay in storage units. Particularly intriguing are the strange color combinations used in the décor—pale lime green mixed with cream, orange, cruise-ship blue, muddy greens, powder pink, and silver. These colors can be found in vintage thirties clothing but are not what we normally reach for today in clothing or decoration. Even Brown found the sludge green ceiling in the bathroom a bit too

The Art Decoesque painted glass ceiling is lit from above, making a startling entrance to the apartment. Lucian Bernhard's flamingo pink and glossy black color scheme has been maintained by the present owner, who added the edge of red on the built-in hall table and bench. The myriad locks, however, are strictly New York today!

The living room includes a built-in sideboard designed by Bernhard. Above it is a 1911 Bernhard poster. A large nineteenth-century Chinese vase that Bernhard placed here probably inspired the yellow trim color and niche with overhead shelf. The shelf holds a collection of early-twentieth-century pottery and glass. Between the candlesticks is a 1908 Austrian vase designed by Georg Klimt, brother of painter Gustav Klimt.

A shelf above a group of filing cabinets in the sitting room holds a built-in Bernhard electric clock.

alien, and changed it to a dark gray blue. It is still in keeping with the original dark-ceiling concept, though slightly more acceptable to our late-twentieth-century eyes. The same ceiling color continues through a small closet-lined passageway and the study. The kitchen was originally a symphony in mud browns—not too conducive to our ideas of cuisine—so the cupboards were given an uplifting coat of Chinese red. Lucian Bernhard would have approved.

Bernhard's designing talents extended to other aspects of decoration. He constructed unique covers for the radiators and a cover for an early air conditioner into which he installed an electric light. In the living room, where he held conferences, six-inch-wide, shoulder-height shelves were built on opposite walls. They had several deep grooves in their upper surfaces, which made it easy to display constantly changing design ideas, pictures, layouts, and so forth. Brown now uses them to show rare early Bernhard posters. Like Bernard, he hangs no pictures on the walls.

Other Bernhard details include the placement of mirrors—sometimes catty-cornered—to catch unusual reflections. Brown has retained them all.

Bernhard invented his own crown moldings in certain places, using a series of dowel rods split through the center and attached to the wall. Drawer knobs are of dowels, and many are in contrasting colors.

When the building was renovated, the plan included replacing all the original metal-framed, small-paned windows with larger, more contemporary panes of glass. Brown requested that the windows be left as they were because the earlier style was very much a part of the apartment's concept. Luckily, this request was granted.

Despite his term of residence, Brown is still discovering ingeniously placed drawers or tucked-away cupboards, some yielding Bernhard memorabilia. He has uncovered hidden caches of original drawings—including fashion croquis—and sketches of advertising logos for well-known companies such as AMOCO, a stack of logo ideas fit into a specially designed holder for presentation, miniposters, palettes, crayons, pastels, boxes of color samples, bills, newspaper clippings, and personal letters—some from other well-known typographers. These discoveries make living in the apartment a continuing adventure.

The large living room overlooks 86th Street. The chairs, coffee table, bookshelves, leather-covered sofa, and the ample storage unit behind the sofa were designed by Bernhard. Grooved shelves on the walls are also original, designed to display layouts to clients. They are now useful for showing large drawings and paintings, such as these early Bernhard posters.

A small sitting room (believed to have been Bernhard's design office) adjoins the living room. In the foreground can be seen the very thirties-looking dowel drawer handles of the storage unit that backs the living room sofa. The sitting room sofa, upholstered in wide-wale corduroy, snuggles in a matching lined niche. The shelf above holds early-twentieth-century Austrian pottery and, on the extreme left, a vase designed by Bernhard in the thirties. Built-in filing cabinets, drawers, and shelves—and even the upholstery fabric—are all part of the original Bernhard design.

In Bernhard's day, this kitchen was painted in very somber colors, but today's owner selected a more cheerful Chinese red. The cupboards are all original.

HIGH CAMP LOFT

Designer Frederick Norton has lived in a full-floor loft on Manhattan's Lower West Side since 1976. Like many loft dwellers in this town where square footage is at a premium, he has never regretted his decision to sacrifice fashionable location for plenty of space.

One block long, Renwick Street is wedged between Spring and Canal streets near the Hudson River, an area not so much SoHo as "So So," as Bette Midler—who owns a loft in the neighborhood—quips. The street was named after a notable Columbia University professor of physics, a philanthropist and founder of the Mercantile Society. He was also the father of one of New York's best-known nineteenth-century architects, James Renwick, designer of Gothic Revival Grace Church and St. Patrick's Cathedral.

During the nineteenth century Renwick Street consisted of two-and-a-half-story single-family houses. As commerce moved north, these houses gradually gave way to industrial buildings and towering warehouses. By 1900 it was an industrial area. Luckily, three surviving charming, early-nineteenth-century houses can be seen from Norton's window.

During the 1960s, artists and designers, forced by high rents to leave the Village, began moving into lower Manhattan's industrial buildings, using them first as studios, then—often illegally—as residences. Many ingeniously hid their possessions behind false bookcases until strict fire department laws were changed and the buildings were deemed suitable as apartments.

The building Frederick Norton lives in was built around 1890 as a glue factory, to serve the many printing firms in the neighborhood. Even today printing is an important local trade. The original building was only six floors high, but as elevators became more prevalent, two more floors were added. On Norton's floor, the seventh, traces of this conversion can still be found.

Later the building was taken over by the Globe Storage and Moving Company. Its name can still be seen painted high up on one of the exterior brick walls. By this time the nearby docks were busy with cargo and passengers; the Holland-America line berthed the *Rotterdam* and the *Amsterdam* at neighboring Morton Street until the beginning of the 1970s.

When the loft-living laws were changed in the late 1960s, the building became residential. It was bought by X-rated movie star Jennifer Wells. She lived in the Norton loft. Now the building is a cooperative, with different tenants occupying each floor.

Norton, who shares his loft with one other person and three cats, is an interior designer. He has created a unique niche for himself as a decorator of beauty salons. He is a consultant to Glemby, a company that operates beauty salons in department and women's specialty stores internationally. This occupation has had a more than subliminal effect on his own dwelling place. When salons are disbanded, remodeled, or renovated, guess who gets first choice of the discarded chandeliers?

The mood of Norton's apartment is "tongue-in-chic," with Liberace overtones, as first seen in the crude warehouse elevator, unexpectedly furnished with a floral-design carpet, a paisley-upholstered banquette, and a pedestal table holding a plant. There is a deft, outrageous wit to the way one is greeted by a glittery chandelier hung from the ceiling next to sprinkler pipes that track across the loft's space. Though the area is big, the loft

An industrial elevator sports a removable carpet (from Stark), a banquette upholstered in paisley fabric from Cowtan & Tout, and a side table with a plant. A neighbor's dog, Tramp, finds it a comfortable way to go.

possesses unity, dictated by the décor: Prussian blue wall-to-wall industrial carpeting covers what were the beat-up concrete floors; ceilings and trendy seventies "high-tack" exposed pipes, wires, and grids have been painted to match gray moiré-upholstered walls. The apartment enjoys the luxury of light on three sides; window shades of black plastic mesh, or perforated blinds, cut the glare.

With a vast expanse to fill, Norton has arranged a series of small conversational groups, like rooms without walls. Oriental rugs tie the seating arrangements together. The effect is warm and inviting. Two or two hundred people could be equally well accommodated. Lighting consists of the startling crystal chandeliers, contemporary Italian "Frisbi" fixtures from Atelier International, and no-nonsense track lighting fixed to exposed beams. Furnishings range from good nineteenth-century furniture and serviceable reproductions to contemporary granite-topped tables on steel and "haute junque."

The most elaborate renovations—"a real gut job"—took place in the kitchen area. Norton enlarged the previous kitchen to include a wall of shelves and storage units and two long counters that separate it from the dining area. These counters are covered with mist gray laminate to blend with the overall scheme, and can be used as table or bar. Here and around the nearby dining table, the floor is covered with American Olean mosaic tile set in a random pattern, impervious to inevitable spills. New ranges, dishwasher, and refrigerators were installed.

The fixtures in one bathroom were a legacy from movie queen Jennifer Wells. They are an

In the foyer a chandelier—from Detroit department store J. L. Hudson—hangs above an 1880s pedestal table with tooled leather top. On it are bronze Russian soldiers and various pieces of English, American, and Finnish glass. Vertically quilted, metalized charcoal upholstery fabric hides a rough wall and provides a foil for Kevin Teare's painting *Motorcade Route with Pillbox Hat*, 1982. An Ishak runner leads into the living room area. The love seat and chair are a set, American, circa 1890.

The original loft ceiling has been painted to match the moiré wall upholstery. The large living room is divided into conversational groups, using an amusing and eclectic mix of antique, reproduction, and thrift-shop furniture. In the foreground, an American Gothic armchair and French reproduction armchairs, up-holstered in Jack Lenor Larsen fabrics, surround a contemporary chrome-base table with ebony gloss laminate top. All sit on a 1920s Chinese carpet. An 1885 Chinese covered bowl garnishes the table.

aggressive sixties lime green, so Norton deliberately played off the campiness with rose pink and a wealth of mirrors.

Norton's various accumulations have been arranged with great skill and sleight-of-hand. One corner becomes a library full of books on many subjects, including art, history, and decoration,

stacked in adroit piles almost like pieces of furniture. Here and there cupboards are filled with glass objects—one a regular glass menagerie—or topped with Chinese pots. Each tablescape or corner tends to be more of a display job than serious décor but the eye always lingers on the folly and is amused.

A small and simple bedroom painted in pansy blue appears enlarged by the mirrored wall. Antique carpet fragments made into pillows are used as a headboard. The bedspread is cotton fabric from Kravet. Side chairs upholstered in green velvet are English Chippendale reproductions, circa 1880. A collection of Plexiglas prisms adorns the table.

A glass-topped dining table rests on bamboo supports. Instead of a tablecloth, dark red velvet runners flank an embroidered Chinese scarf. The table is set with a mixture of old Tiffany pieces, Edwardian silver plate, and sterling. An adapted chandelier—part of which came from a St. Louis beauty salon and part from Bergdorf Goodman in New York—is reflected in a mirror discarded from a renovation job.

EAST SIDE CREATURE COMFORTS

The side streets off Park, Fifth, and Madison avenues on the Upper East Side of Manhattan are lined with houses in a variety of styles popular in the late nineteenth and early twentieth centuries. There are variations on the Georgian manor, the Italianate palazzo, and the Beaux-Arts mansion, all coexisting in agreeable and interesting juxtaposition. As Paul Goldberger says in *New York: The City Observed*, "... it is all of history spread out as in a catalogue so that each millionaire might be able to take his pick, and yet it is all New York, too, an eclectic jumble that maintains a clear and strong sense of continuity and sense of place." The *really* grandiose mansions were built right on Fifth and Park avenues at this time as well, but they were all too frequently torn down in the 1920s, '30s, and '40s to make room for multistoried, luxury apartment buildings. Town houses on the side streets were never quite as palatial, and have generally survived because they didn't sit on such developable real estate. By today's standards, however, many town houses in this area are so stately they are owned by institutions rather than by single families, for whom they were designed.

Stephen and Cathy Graham needed to find the right house to start their married life. Cathy, an illustrator, had been living the life of an artist in a SoHo loft. Stephen is a theater producer, and also the founder and chief board member of the New York Theater Workshop—a ten-year-old organization that stages new plays and encourages new directors. In 1987, after a long search, the Grahams found a warm, human-scale, ivy-covered, Georgian-inspired town house on the Upper East Side and it suited them to perfection.

As they set about feathering their new nest,

they discovered that it is not easy to plunge into the competitive world of what one might call grown-up decorating. In America, unlike Europe, access to all the most splendid sources—including fabrics and wallpapers—is possible only through an architect or decorator. This is the main reason so many Americans—New Yorkers in particular—no matter how confident or stylish their personal taste, are compelled to turn to professional designers. For the Grahams there was considerable start and stop at the beginning before they found the right decorator for them, Brian McCarthy of Parish-Hadley.

By the time McCarthy inherited the job, the Grahams had made many expeditions to Europe—England, in particular—collecting exemplary furnishings for the house. "Lots of very good stuff," acknowledges McCarthy. He also feels they have managed to preserve—probably because of their careers in the arts—a wonderfully fresh, unusually youthful and casual quality to their house, despite its setting in the midst of Upper East Side formality.

In the vestibule it is instantly apparent that someone here is mad about flowers. The sunken tray of the vestibule table is crammed with a delightful array of colorful blossoms. In the entrance hall, six good-looking, curious, and very friendly cats converge to check out visitors. Named Molly, Rhoda, Pinky, Kaylyn, Betty, and Ernie, they are all very much a part of the family. The marble-floored hall has walls hand-painted by Robert Jackson in a Chinese-inspired design of trees, blossoms, and birds. Several of the cats are portrayed, and more are to be added. Two carved and gilded Chinese Chippendale mirrors look thoroughly at home here. One is placed over a Regency hall table designed in a Brighton Pavilion fantasy-Chinese style; the table is flanked by stone lions found at an English

A 1920s mirrored chest of drawers found at Mallets, Bourdon House, in London sits in the hall beneath a carved gilt English chinoiserie looking glass. Reflected in it are the doors leading to the dining room. The hall walls were painted by Robert Jackson, who included some of the family cats in the Chinese-style design.

antique statuary auction; the other mirror hangs above a deliciously distressed, mirrored bureau with brass drawer pulls, made in the 1920s and found at Mallets, Bourdon House, in London. On it pots of hydrangeas flank a small metal trough filled with pale, pink-tinged roses and supported by two classically draped Art Nouveau–ish ladies.

The source of this profusion of flowers can be found by descending a staircase leading from the hall to the basement, where Cathy has installed a florist's refrigerator that is always stocked with seasonal flora. Stephen is not far away. A rock drummer manqué, he practices in a specially sound-

proofed basement room. "We both spend a great deal of time down there," Cathy says.

Also off the hall is the dining room, reached through glass-paned doors installed by the Grahams. Soft-colored, striped curtains frame French windows that open onto a back garden, where the Grahams have constructed a stylish house for the neighborhood's stray cats. At a mere call from the dining room, cats of all sizes and colors emerge from this house, for all the world like the children who run out from beneath the skirts of Mother Ginger in *The Nutcracker* ballet. The wonder is how they all fit into such a tiny space. On cold nights the cats'

A Bessarabian carpet sets the tone of the living room. Three curtained windows overlook the back garden. On the wall is *Silver* by nineteenth-century English painter Albert Moore. Three of the family cats are in evidence: Betty, on the pink armchair; Pinky, on the small chair; and Molly, on the yellow armchair.

The library boasts an exemplary eighteenth-century Carlton House desk. Above it is a painting of a waterfall by Western landscapist Thomas Moran. Beneath the wall sconces are two anonymous nautical paintings from Bardith, New York.

In the library, Clarence House chintz curtains and upholstery complement the Persian carpet from Doris Leslie Blau. Between the windows a William Blake watercolor hangs above a case clock from Sotheby's, New York. The sofa is covered in striated coral velvet and adorned with antique needlepoint cushions. Dark green paint lines the bookcases.

villa is warmed by a heat lamp that glows in the dark. The feline antics provide endless diversion for the Grahams, who not only name and feed all the strays but also have them spayed and neutered. The somewhat more privileged indoor cats are not allowed to mingle with the strays, much as they'd like to, but can signal to them through the glass doors.

An attractive and welcoming kitchen leads off the hall. Casual meals are served at a table by a window overlooking the street. The white country floor tiles were already in place when the Grahams moved in but they installed butcher block counters and white cupboards.

On the floor above, a landing boasts a grand piano. Behind it is a coromandel screen, which will eventually be replaced by bookcases.

A sunny yellow permeates the living room, which is dominated by three tall windows with swagged curtains. A flower-patterned Bessarabian carpet covers the floor. Cream and yellow damask-upholstered sofas and armchairs mix well with coral padded, oval-backed Hepplewhite chairs, all of which provide comfortable berths for the cats. An English sewing box in front of the central window serves as a table for a lamp, decorative objects, and flowers. A large gilt Chippendale looking glass complements Canton jars and a flower-filled bowl on the mantel. Next to the fireplace is a decorative watercolor by contemporary British artist Glynn Boyd Harte, a staunch member of the Georgian Group. Opposite the fireplace hangs Albert Moore's *Silver*, a painting of a woman that was exhibited at the Royal Academy in 1886. A smaller painting by the same artist sits on a nearby table. An English lacquered games table from the Pelham Galleries holds a painting, *Leda and the Swan*, found in a country antique shop, as well as photographs and a nineteenth-century French clock. Antique needlepoint cushions embellish sofas and chairs, and there are fresh flowers everywhere.

A similar elegant coziness prevails in the library, where a flowered chintz from Clarence House is used for the curtains and two armchairs. Another print, of flowers and animals, covers an ottoman. The sofa is upholstered in striated coral velvet. Anchoring the room is a Persian carpet from Doris Leslie Blau. The bookcases were already in the room when the Grahams moved in, but what finally made them work, Cathy contends, was McCarthy's classic use of dark green paint to line them. Interspersed among the books are decorative objects and small paintings, including two—one of an apple and the other of a half-peeled orange—by Robert Kulicke, the inventor of the Kulicke picture frame. A William Blake watercolor hangs over an English case clock found at Sotheby's, New York. Next to it is a superb English celestial globe with a compass set into the base of its wooden stand. A distinguished Carlton House desk—found at a Christie's sale—sits under a painting of a spectacular waterfall by Thomas

Moran (1837–1926), who is often cited as the most masterful of Western landscape painters, with his three artist brothers closely rivaling his skill. Another carved and gilded Chippendale mirror, this one embellished with griffins, hangs over the mantelpiece. As in the living room, antique needlepoint cushions and fresh flowers provide pleasing accents.

Off the library is a tiny bar lined with a 1940s wallpaper that Cathy discovered and was anxious to use. She thought that this paper, with its pink elephants and champagne bubbles on a dark blue ground, might not be to Parish-Hadley's very proper taste, but Brian McCarthy loved it and suggested shellacking it to a high gloss, thereby transforming it into an amusing frivolity.

On the floor above, more flowered chintz ornaments the master bedroom, which adjoins a pink-toned bathroom with stippled walls, white tiles, and a swagged wallpaper border. Here Cathy indulges her love of miniature objects: tiny perfume

In Cathy Graham's bathroom the walls have been sponged in a warm pink beige and embellished with a swagged wallpaper border. Tiny decorative framed pictures and a doll's tea set ornament the room. The master bedroom can be seen through the door.

bottles, small, decorative framed pictures, and a doll's tea set. Another bathroom and Stephen's office completes this floor.

A guest room can be found on the fourth floor. On the floor above that is the media room, so named because Stephen, a film addict, has filled one whole wall of shelves with his alphabetically arranged video cassettes. Dark green walls, a mahogany mantel, solid-color curtains, and sisal matting impart a masculine atmosphere to the room. Softening touches are supplied by a nineteenth-century English needlepoint rug partially covering the matting and comfortable furniture upholstered in a rose-patterned Colefax & Fowler chintz. The walls are studded with family photographs and the mantel supports a big bowl of flowers flanked by two handsome carved wooden horses found by Parish-Hadley.

Off the second guest room on this floor is a bathroom lined with another of Cathy's whimsical wallpapers from the 1940s. It depicts strutting French poodles on a mint green ground.

Cathy's studio, with its good natural light and simple white lace curtains, overlooks the back garden. The walls have been kept plain and pale, the floor is bleached, and the only distractions are a wealth of flowers and the temptation to peer outside and check on the neighborhood cats.

Though the Grahams say their house is still a work in progress, they have created a nice balance between the traditional chintz-and-needlepoint décor of the family rooms and the more functional décor of the rooms in which they pursue their artistic endeavors. Constantly enlivened by fresh flowers and countless cats, this town house is truly a place of creature comforts.

At the top of the house is the media room, where a wall of shelves holds a large selection of videos. Photographs of family and friends are hung on the dark green walls. Above the wooden mantel is an English mirror found by Parish-Hadley. The sisal matting is partly covered by an English needlepoint rug. The chintz is from Colefax & Fowler.

STATEN ISLAND VICTORIAN

To many people New York means Manhattan. But New York City, of course, consists of five boroughs. The most removed of them all is Staten Island, which, because of its location, looks as if it belongs more to New Jersey than to New York. At one point in history it almost did. When the English seized New Amsterdam in 1664, the island became part of the province of New York. The proprietors of New Jersey protested, and as tradition has it, the dispute was settled by a race around the island, which was won by a Captain Christopher Billopp for New York. The British named the island Richmond after the duke of Richmond, a son of Charles II. At the same time it retained the original Dutch name of Staten Eylandt, in honor of the States General of the Netherlands. Richmond is still the official name of the county, but within it is the Borough of Staten Island.

After Staten Island was colonized, farms and, gradually, villages were established. To this day it retains a far more rural ambience than the other boroughs and many Staten Islanders are proud of the distinction. Indeed, there has long been talk of the island seceding from New York City. Until the 1964 opening of the Verrazano-Narrows Bridge the only means of transportation was the Staten Island ferry—still the best bargain in town at twenty-five cents there and back! Few people who take the trip, however, bother to explore the island.

By the 1830s, Staten Island had become a fashionable bathing resort. New Brighton, situated close to the ferry dock and named in honor of Brighton, England, the Prince Regent's seaside playground, became *the* place for affluent Staten Islanders, such as the Comstocks, Rianhards, Phelps-Stokes, Walkers, and Wimans, to live in grand style.

Though it was a year-round community, some New Yorkers lived there only during summer, so it predated Newport, Rhode Island, as a stylish place for sumptuous "cottages." During the nineteenth-century development of the island, houses were built either in vernacular, mostly rural form, or, more modishly, in Federal, Greek Revival, Gothic Revival, Italianate, Stick, or Eclectic style.

One Pendleton Place in New Brighton is one of the few surviving houses in the Gothic Revival style. Built in 1860, the house now serves as an unofficial rectory for the parish of the community's Christ Church. It is shared by the Reverend John H. Walsted and Gerald Keucher, a volunteer church worker who handles the accounts of the Staten Island Institute of Arts and Sciences, and Mr. Keucher's mother, Martha.

The house has an interesting history. In an area that had become highly desirable by the mid-nineteenth century, some ten acres were acquired by William S. Pendleton, a wealthy developer, who built seven houses on the property. For many years Pendleton Place was a private street, situated close to Hamilton Park, a smart section full of big mansions and estates. The builder, who came from Boston, was responsible for introducing commercial lithography to the New York area and worked with the well-known printmakers Currier and Ives.

The first people to move into One Pendleton Place were the affluent Staten Island Rianhard family. An engraving of the house, labeled "Residence of T. M. Rianhard, Esq.," appeared as a frontispiece in the *Horticulturalist* magazine in 1862. (This engraving is now reproduced on the present owners' stationery.) An accompanying article entitled "How to Build Your Country Houses," by architect Charles Duggin, describes the arrangement of rooms, shows

An 1850 hall tree in the vestibule stands on a floor made up of eight varieties of wood. The original etched-glass windows and the beveled glass of the front door have survived for 130 years. All the hardware, however, is obviously contemporary. The dog doorstop is early twentieth century.

a floor plan, discusses the construction and finish, and quotes a building estimate of $6,500 without the cost of furnace, mantels, grates, and plumbing. The house must have been quite up-to-date, for it included an indoor bathroom, a basement washroom, and a kitchen "fitted with every convenience such as range, boiler, dresser, closet, etc." Hints were offered for interior decoration. Duggin suggests that from a hall arch "could be suspended curtains, which, if hung in festoons and gathered up gracefully, would tend much to enhance the appearance of the hall. With the arch and curtains this space could still be appropriated as a library or snuggery, to be enclosed by the drapery when in use."

The Rianhards rented the house. Most likely by 1869, and certainly by 1874, Pendleton himself lived here, and the house remained in the hands of the Pendleton family until it was sold to Wilbur Wirtz Mills and his family around 1920. Mills was Commissioner of Ports and Terminals for the City of New York. He entertained many political figures, including Mayor La Guardia, who took the ferry trip to dine here.

Despite its twenty-two rooms on four floors, sturdy construction, and illustrious guests, the house was never considered particularly grand by neighborhood standards. Its comparative modesty and location on a small, irregular, one-acre hill, however, are the reasons for its survival. During the twentieth century, and especially just after the 1929 crash, many of the mansion owners—those on Staten Island were especially hard hit—found themselves unable to heat their houses or pay for servants. The large estates on which these mansions stood were coveted by developers, who bought them during the Depression and divided them into small lots. One Pendleton Place was never that desirable nor was the land it stood on easy to divide. Thankfully, it was bypassed by "progress."

Episcopal networking brought the present owners to the house. After meeting in a Manhattan church in 1977, Walsted and Keucher discovered that they shared an interest in old houses. In 1980 they bought an abandoned wreck of a house in New Brighton and fixed it up. Soon they wanted to upgrade their residence. Keucher had formulated

Perched on a grassy rise, this twenty-two-room 1860 Gothic Revival villa not only has survived intact but is today in use as the unofficial rectory for the parish of Christ Church, New Brighton, on Staten Island.

The snuggery at the end of the hall shows a tilt-top table and small nineteenth-century chest from an old Staten Island family. The hooked rug was made in Indiana by Jerry Keucher's great-grandmother. The eighteenth-century New England highboy displays a collection of art glass, Depression glass, and cut glass. The looking glass and candle stand have been in place since early in the house's history.

a three-part wish list: He wanted a house with interesting room arrangements, a tower, and a single-digit address. Passing by One Pendleton Place, barely visible behind a thick growth of trees and shrubbery, he realized it satisfied all three wishes. By coincidence, its owner sang in St. Thomas's Fifth Avenue choir with Keucher's former next-door neighbor, who was in real estate, so Jerry was the first to know the house was going up for sale. Keucher and Walsted made an offer and the house was theirs even before it could be listed on the market. In 1983 they moved in, and the same year, John Walsted was called as Rector of Christ Church, New Brighton.

When Keucher and Walsted bought One Pendleton Place, the house was run-down. Some of the trees had to be cut away (to the regret of Martha Keucher) to restore a driveway leading to the front door, and shrubs were trimmed back. Flowers have been planted in formal Victorian bedded style with urns and statues placed at focal points. Stone steps lead up to the front door and a wide veranda wraps around one end of the house. Tall, round-topped, etched windows are set into

double vestibule doors. The vestibule opens onto both the porch and the central entrance hall. The floor in the vestibule is made up of eight varieties of wood arranged in contrasting stripes as a sort of sampler. In front of the fireplace in the central hall, contrasting wood has been inlaid to imitate a hearth mat. Similar attention has been paid to the wood flooring throughout the house; for instance, in the library (called the sitting room in the original plans) an elaborate Greek-key motif has been worked around the border of the room. This room seems to have been the most formal and detailed in the house. Its elaborate marble fireplace depicts shells and bunches of grapes, and a curved plaster arch supported by ancones outlines the bay window.

The hall runs the length of the house. There's a parlor leading off to the right, and the library/ sitting room, stairs, and dining room to the left. Keucher and Walsted did not take Duggin's advice and add "drapery," but the far end of the hall makes a cozy snuggery all the same. Too small an area for a serious twentieth-century reader's library, the nook currently contains a marvelous eighteenth-century highboy, a grandfather clock, two rocking chairs, a tilt-top pedestal table, a small nineteenth-century chest, and an almost-ceiling-height corner looking glass and candle stand.

On a Duncan Phyfe transition-period sideboard are covered cheese dishes, a late-eighteenth-century Meissen cake stand, candlesticks with crocheted *bobèches*, and an 1820s flint glass fruit bowl. The egg tempera pictures on the wall are all Father Walsted's work.

On the table are Indian Tree–patterned Spode plates. The wood napkin rings are 1920s souvenirs from Washington, D.C. They are numbered for various family members and belonged to Keucher's grandmother in Indiana, as did the glass water pitchers and goblets.

The house was originally heated by coal fires. In the 1880s, central heating—then an innovation—was installed. Radiators from this time are still in place and working. From its inception, however, the house had indoor plumbing, which was very modern for 1860. It even boasted an upstairs bathroom, though the present tub was added recently—it came, rather suitably, from a nearby Roman Catholic rectory. There was probably another bathroom downstairs for servants.

In the dining room the original built-in diamond-paned cupboards are still in use. Pink moiré curtains by New York decorator Elizabeth Fanuzzi soften the windows. A huge china cabinet is on permanent loan from a friend whose rooms are too small for it.

The kitchen, despite its having "every convenience" of 1860, has been drastically altered to serve today's needs. A central island contains work counters and storage space, and what was once a pantry has now become an informal eating area.

The rest of the house remains basically as it was in Pendleton's day. One piece of furniture, an 1850s spool chair, belonged to the Pendletons while they lived here. Though some parts are missing from the banister, most of the house has been restored into fairly good shape. Of the twenty-two rooms, many are bedrooms. One room is Father Walsted's studio, where, using traditional egg tempera, he paints icons, many for religious institutions. Throughout the house one finds these vivid, gold-touched images, executed in accordance with the strict conventions of Byzantine and Russian icon painting. Walsted is also responsible for various faux malachite lamp bases and other painted decorative details.

The house today has no more pretensions to grandeur than it did at the time of its construction. It is part home and part working place, a welcoming, open residence with people coming in and out all day on parish or personal business. Compared with a decorated Park Avenue apartment, it radiates unintimidating ease and a pleasant dowdiness. Well-loved, it is full of a much-used mixture of family accumulations, bits and pieces found at church bazaars, and furniture from old Staten Island families.

The tower room at the top of the house is surrounded by windows. Sun-bleached wicker, patchwork cushions, and the last roses of summer combine to make it a perfect spot to read or ruminate.

HOTEL DES ARTISTES

Around the time of World War I, a group of about forty artists living in New York banded together and decided to build an apartment building designed to suit their needs. A plot was bought on West 67th Street before there were any other large buildings on this narrow thoroughfare. Architect George Mort Pollard designed the structure using tudoresque motifs, including ogee arches over the central windows on the stone facade and fanciful carved busts depicting "the arts." The result was the Hotel des Artistes, which is not a hotel at all, though in the early days it provided many of the services of one.

Inside, medieval-inspired details abound, from the lobby's wood-beamed ceiling to the Gothic chairs that flank the elaborate metal-doored elevator. Above the elevator entrance is a mural by Corey Kilvert depicting New York Harbor in the seventeenth century. An early brochure for the building shows a swimming pool and mentions a gymnasium and handball court. A small theater and a ballroom were available for "lectures, dances, theatricals, concerts, recitals, etc." These two rooms still exist but are about to be restored—one as an art gallery, and the other as an extension of the street level Café des Artistes, one of New York's best-loved restaurants. It boasts bucolic murals of naked ladies painted by commercial artist Howard Chandler Christy. In the early days, this restaurant was known as the coffee room and bar. A far more substantial kitchen that at one point employed seventeen French chefs and prepared meals to order for the occupants has long since been converted into apartments.

Other conveniences the hotel used to offer included a riding school across the street (now an ABC-TV building)—a stone's throw from Central Park—valet service, maid service (at 50 cents an hour), a beauty parlor, and a twenty-four-hour switchboard. This last amenity remains.

Most of the apartments have double-height living rooms, balcony bedrooms, and big windows, many of them with the "north light" ideal for painters and sculptors. They come in various sizes: studios with sleeping balconies, duplexes, and triplexes. Some have stone fireplaces and Gothic detailing.

The 1928 brochure lists some of the prominent people "who have made their home in this building." Though many are no longer household names, the list includes Howard Chandler Christy himself, Noel Coward, Fannie Hurst, Heywood Hale Broun, William Powell, Edna Ferber, painters Augustus John and Norman Rockwell, opera singer Lawrence Tibbett, bandleader Paul Whiteman, Alexander Woolcott, actress Zasu Pitts, Alla Nazimova, Stanley Mortimer, and Rudolf Valentino and his wife, Natasha Rambova, who, before adopting this more exotic name, was Winifred Shaughnessy.

The pioneering American dancer Isadora Duncan lived here, and during her residence she posed for American painter Arthur B. Davies. Today, in the same apartment where she was painted, another artist, Dean Fausett, resides. He is now the owner of Davies's preliminary charcoal sketch of Isadora. Fausett has lived in the building longer than most. His apartment comprises a gigantic living room and a two-bedroom floor above; he also owns a three-bedroom apartment next door—painted in Pompeian style—which he rents out to a friend. Fausett installed mirrored doors between the two apartments that can be opened to throw musical soirées for up to a hundred and fifty people. The twenty-foot ceilings provide excellent acoustics.

Leading off the living room under a carved-wood pediment is the "Greek" dining room. Greek-key motifs decorate the lamp shades, outline the painted floor, and form the backs of the metal klismos chairs by Richard Sandford.

Rambova and Rudolf Valentino, though married, did not share the same apartment in the Hotel des Artistes. Valentino lived with his butler in what is now Dean Fausett's apartment. His meals were prepared in the kitchen downstairs, sent up on the dumbwaiter, and served by the butler. The apartment has two staircases leading to the bedroom balcony—one for the owner, and one leading from the entrance hall to be used more discreetly by the servant.

Dean Fausett is exactly the type of person for whom the building was intended. As a young man, he came to New York to work with his older artist brother, Lyn Fausett, a prominent muralist who became president of the Art Students' League. Dean's skills in the visual arts range from drawing and painting portraits and landscapes (Wildenstein is his gallery) to sculpture and set design. He is even credited with the rediscovery of a unique drafting device based on an ancient abacus chart that speedily transforms architectural plans into three-dimensional drawings, thus saving weeks of valuable time. His many achievements include being president of the National Society of Mural Painters as well as founder and fund-raiser for the Southern Vermont Art Center in Manchester, Vermont.

As Paul Goldberger describes them, the apartments in des Artistes "all look as if they were designed as sets for *La Bohème*, and they are a special category of New York housing unto themselves." This is true of Dean Fausett's and he would be the first to say he liked it that way. The sheer scale of the double-height rooms is startling and theatrical. To work here, furniture has to be oversized, and a certain amount of drama in the décor also helps. Most of Fausett's furniture is deliberately stagy, such as a mock-medieval Dante chair. All the fancy paint finishes—faux bois, lacquering, porphyry, marbleizing, and antiquing—in both apartments were done by him.

When Fausett bought his apartment, there was a window in the entrance hall. It overlooked a rather dismal view of the fire escape, so Fausett closed it off and created a decorative niche that now holds an eleventh-century figure flanked by two antique bronze vessels. A marble-topped table in a corner of the hall serves as his writing desk. A carved mahogany table with griffins was once a prized possession of Antoinette Perry, for whom Broadway's Tony Awards are named.

The vast living room has been made particularly

In the living room the antiqued-wood pilasters and carved, solid mahogany supports, capitals, and pediment came from a church in New Orleans. On the far wall is a view of Venice after a thunderstorm painted by Dean Fausett. It is flanked by Venetian carved-and-gilded mirrors set on panels of antique Italian damask bordered with antique braid.

In the master bedroom, swags of bullion-fringed antique fabric have been theatrically draped and held with gold cord and tassels at the head of the bed. A metal crown once decorated the apex. Equestrian prints hang on either side of the bed. The damask-covered door is studded with "jewels" in the center of each motif. A hand-crocheted afghan lies on the bed.

The "Florentine" bathroom—so called because the ceramic tiles came from Florence—features a niche that holds a sculptural figure of Venus on the half shell. A custom-made Vermont-marble-topped washstand complements the gold-painted basin and dolphin faucets.

spectacular by the application of solid, carved mahogany architectural details—pilasters, capitals, ancones (S-shaped supports), and a pediment—all from an eighteenth-century church in New Orleans. To blend them in, Fausett gave them a subtle Italianesque antique finish. Also from New Orleans is a French chandelier made with pear-shaped Baccarat crystal drops. Its height—nine feet from top to bottom—is far too big for the average New York room, but here it fits in brilliantly. Beneath the balcony a comfortable sofa nestles against a mirror that reflects much of the room. Beige silk Venetian damask with a heavy bullion fringe has been used to soften and cover cupboards and a door leading into the next apartment. In front of the triple-height windows is a giant table. For fund-raising parties, it can accommodate a Bacchanalian buffet. Its surface is covered with antique damask protected by glass. On the wall facing the balcony are two ornately carved and gilded Venetian mirrors hung on panels of antique damask bordered with braid. They flank a large painting of Venice by Dean Fausett and, above it, a Florentine masterpiece. Smaller pictures— such as Fausett's portrait of the late conductor Eugene Ormandy and a drawing of ballet costumes by set designer Eugene Berman—share another wall with the two-faced stem of an Attic urn from the Greek city of Aphrodisia and a deep-toned portrait of Titian above an Italian mahogany cabinet.

The dining room, entered under the wooden church pediment, is in striking contrast to the muted colors of the living room. Here the walls are lacquered brilliant red, and the accents are black and white with white taffeta draperies. The recurring motif is the Greek key. Greek-key braid edges the lamp shades, a Greek-key design borders the painted floor, and the same motif is echoed in the backs of black cast-metal chairs by Richard Sandford, a designer of the 1930s and 1940s, famous for his miniature period rooms. Classically shaped pottery is arranged on shelves at the far end of the dining room, hiding another view of the fire escape. Classical drawings are surrounded by gold-studded frames. A screen conceals the doorway into the small, bachelor-styled kitchen.

The stairs, covered with celery-colored carpet, lead up to the balcony. Three rooms lead off of it:

a small guest room with a single bed, the "Florentine" bathroom, and the master bedroom.

Theatrical draping decorates the bed in the master bedroom. Antique brocade lines the back wall, red corduroy covers the headboard, and plush is used for the curtains. In this room, a Fausett autumn landscape hangs over the fireplace, which is truly theatrical—a nonfunctional leftover from a stage set that Mr. Fausett worked on. The bathroom is equally whimsical, with a sculpture of Venus rising from the sea, flanked by bronze classic columns, dolphin faucets on the Greek-key-decorated washbasin, and swans holding the towels.

Amid these diverse accumulations—rich Italianate details, sleight-of-hand antiquing, and dramatic flourishes, all accompanied by soaring theatrical music—Dean Fausett lives the contented life of a very proper Bohemian.

From the balcony, which has served as an art gallery for Fausett's prize-winning paintings, can be seen the huge windows designed for the "artistes'" studios. The Baccarat crystal chandelier, nine feet from top to bottom, came from New Orleans. Large-scale, theatrical yet classic furniture has been used in this room.

UPPER EAST SIDE EPHEMERA

Antiques dealer James Robinson left England for America in the 1930s to open a shop specializing in antique silver aimed at the carriage trade. The shop was successful, eventually branching out into jewelry and porcelain. In the 1950s it was sold to Robinson's brother-in-law, Edward Munves, Sr., a New Yorker who had learned the antique furniture trade in England. Mr. Munves, Sr., retained the well-established James Robinson name and moved the store to 12 East 57th Street—New York's most acclaimed street for luxury shopping.

Edward Munves's widow, Barbara, became more and more interested in the antiques business, and eventually opened a shop within James Robinson. It is now James II Galleries. As sources for Georgian silver dried up, nineteenth-century artifacts, which hitherto had not been considered serious antiques, became more meaningful. Her shop set out to serve the wedding-present trade, dealing less in furniture than in small objects. Starting with Victorian silver plate, then expanding into the realm of Victorian colored glass—triggered by finding a Nailsea glass bell—she was able to move into fairly unexplored areas. Now, for instance, she owns a unique collection of early-nineteenth-century colored-glass Nailsea pens, and is currently on the lookout for nineteenth-century baskets of colored-glass fruit.

Although Edward Munves was considerably older than his wife, their marriage was an unusually happy one. When he died on Christmas Eve, 1983, she couldn't bear the idea of continuing to live in their apartment, which held so many memories, and began looking around for a place where she could start life afresh.

One of the first things she did was to separate James II from James Robinson. Now her sole interest is in James II Galleries. She and her daughter Julie Seymour run the aesthetic side of the shop, while another daughter, Cathy Lawrence, helps manage the financial side.

The apartment she found was built in the early part of the century. Having relied for many years on her husband's great knowledge and expertise, Mrs. Munves realized she would need help in decorating the new place, so she turned to her decorator friend Gloria Kaplan of Kaplan Sandercock Associates. They had met years ago when they were students at New York University.

The apartment, designed for a hardworking New York businesswoman, took about a year to complete. Barbara entertains frequently. She also welcomes her children—and *their* children—to stay with her from time to time, so room was made for them. Another requirement was space to display her collections of what she calls "feminine ephemera"—framed cut-paper pictures, paper scrollwork, valentines, bird-feather pictures, sugar tongs, carved ivory objects, gold and silver boxes, needlepoint and beaded cushions, paintings on glass, shoehorns, exotic footwear, and, of course, her exceptional glass pieces.

The elevator hall sets the tone for the uncommon quality of the apartment's contents. A penwork table—rare because this Regency hobby was generally confined to far smaller pieces—sits below a wall of beautifully framed early-eighteenth-century French animal engravings.

An inner hall opens onto a living room, a sitting room, and a dining room. In the living room, furniture is arranged in groups and there are enough unusual collections to start many a conversation. On one wall are fragile cut-paper pictures; one

A Queen Anne mirror reflects a nineteenth-century bull's-eye mirror in this bedroom passage. The hand-blocked wallpaper is from Cowtan & Tout. On the hall table are antique shoehorns and bottles of St. Louis glass made in France in the 1840s.

(much documented) is amazingly still intact from the early eighteenth century. A Sheraton secretary holds a hoard of delicate glass pens. Another collection is of pictures and objects made from tiny paper scrolls—an Italian craft taken up by the English in the eighteenth century—which are surprisingly well preserved in spite of the perishability of the medium. A pair of American Indian beaded moccasins can be seen tucked under a formal Regency

sofa; another exotic pair of shoes sits beneath an armchair; a child's pair lurks under a diminutive Victorian painted papier-mâché chair. This is a running motif throughout the house, begun when Mr. Munves first placed some nineteenth-century bead-embroidered slippers beneath a piece of furniture.

The footwear theme carries into the cozy sitting room. The Munveses found themselves buying

In the living room, a Regency sofa from Mallets in London is covered in striped satin from Scalamandré. Tucked under it are a pair of American Indian moccasins. The carpet is an early-twentieth-century Aubusson from Doris Leslie Blau. A nineteenth-century child's papier-mâché chair is one of a pair. The nineteenth-century screen is Japanese.

A Sheraton secretary (its mate is in the Victoria and Albert Museum in London) holds a unique collection of still usable Nailsea glass pens. In the niches behind are Chelsea and Meissen cane handles.

The Munveses' collection of cut-paper pictures includes a bust of Cicero, the earliest known example of such fine cut-paper work. There are many hidden figures in it—including a naked lady.

antique shoes and sandals wherever they traveled, and their collection ranges from early-eighteenth- to twentieth-century French, English, Persian, Japanese, Indian, and American Indian footwear. The sitting room is an inviting place, with a comfortable sofa to sink into and unwind, sip a drink, or watch television.

Though most of the architectural layout remained intact, major structural changes were made in the bathroom and dressing room area off Mrs. Munves's bedroom. The bathroom became a totally feminine room, swathed in pale blue dotted swiss. Much-needed closet space—the apartment was built, Munves says, in the era of armoires—and a makeup table were worked into previously wasted space.

The kitchen is large and pleasant. As a career woman, Mrs. Munves depends on her full-time housekeeper, Sallie, who is often cooking while grandchildren are using the space as a playroom.

Guest bedrooms include one with a crib for grandchildren. The accompanying bathroom was not remodeled because of its charming old fixtures, but it was transformed by dramatic ceiling-high curtains of dark printed cotton, which was also used to disguise some ugly plumbing.

The success of the apartment lies in the combination of events that have shaped Barbara Munves's life: her relationship with the late Edward Munves, Sr., her early friendship with decorator Gloria Kaplan, her business acumen, and her on-going fascination for off-the-beaten-track antiques.

A sofa nestled into a niche of the sitting room is covered with a wealth of beaded needlepoint cushions and a crocheted throw made by Mrs. Munves's grandmother. The central picture on the red glazed wall is a nineteenth-century newspaper collage (many of the items have special significance to the Munves family) flanked by Victorian ''Penny Plain, Twopence Coloured'' prints of famous actors. The unusual Indian rug, decorated with animals, is from Doris Leslie Blau.

Aubergine glazed walls set the tone for the dining room. Regency chairs surround the table, which holds silver sugar tongs and two late-eighteenth-century Chinese nodding mandarins, made of terra-cotta with porcelain heads. The Chinese lacquered cabinet holds fine blue-and-white Chinese Export porcelain. The Macassar ebony sideboard, inlaid with ivory and satinwood, was designed in neo-Renaissance style by Owen Jones. Its relative is in the Metropolitan Museum. A Regency convex mirror hangs above. Nailsea glass bells are displayed on a pair of Regency torchères.

COLLECTION MONSIEUR AKRAM OJJEH

Monografie Giuseppe Partini

Hogarth's Progress PETER QUENNELL

CARAVAGGIO Howa

AMERICAN FURNITURE 1620 to the present Jonathan L. Fairbanks F. Elizabeth Bidwell Bates

A History of FLOWER ARRAN

Forrest The French Revolution and the Poe

ARCHITECTURE IN THE AGE OF REASON

John Harris

PUG PETER

HUDSON RIVER VILLAS

ITALIAN CASSONI

LADIES' MILE LITERARY

Manhattan's smartest shopping thoroughfares have progressively moved uptown over the last 150 years. Around the mid-nineteenth century 14th Street boasted the finest emporiums, attracting prosperous customers from the surrounding neighborhood. By the end of the century the most affluent shopping site had moved to 23rd Street, later to be eclipsed by 34th Street. It is now centered around 57th Street.

In the 1870s, a nine-block stretch on and around Broadway—an avenue that cuts a diagonal swath across the city's grid—from Union Square at 14th Street to 23rd St was dubbed "Ladies' Mile" because of the grandeur and abundance of its stores. The commercial buildings constructed in the area at that time benefited from new building techniques and other technical innovations. Between 1877 and 1889 alone, telephones, skyscrapers, electric lights, electric trolley cars, subways, automobiles, and elevators had all come into being, transforming and accelerating city life.

But as Manhattan spread north as well as skyward, Ladies' Mile, too, got left behind. The department store buildings were adapted to other uses, many of them becoming offices or manufacturing lofts. For many years Ladies' Mile—the name long since overlooked—dozed as an underused, dowdy area full of cumbersome, dark, and dirty buildings. In the last decade, however, the neighborhood has reawakened. At the forefront of this revival are John and Jane Stubbs, who live and work in a once commercial building overlooking Broadway at 18th Street.

From the Stubbses' corner window can be seen an important chapter in American architecture. As Paul Goldberger says in *New York: The City*

Observed, "These are wonderful, surprising streets . . . an assemblage of fine nineteenth-century buildings." The prototype was the four-story commercial building, with external flourishes influenced by the Beaux Arts style and embellished with French Second Empire details. These were usually substantial buildings, their upper floors used as millinery workrooms, artists' galleries, architects' offices—McKim, Mead & White was just up the way—and photographic studios. Opposite the Stubbses' building is the Gorham silver company's old store, a delicate Victorian trifle built in 1883 and designed by Edward H. Kendall, and a red building that once housed Decca Sheet Music. Nearby is the original Arnold Constable department store, designed by Griffith Thomas, built in 1869 and extended in 1873 and 1877. Not far away is the former Lord & Taylor building, designed by James H. Giles and constructed in 1869–70 of cast iron and glass in the Second Empire manner. Four stories high with an attic, it has been designated a landmark building. Its diagonally set corner tower is crowned with the first mansard roof to be used on a commercial building in the country. Directly across from the Stubbses' floor is the McIntyre Building—a much taller structure. With its ornate base, plain middle shaft soaring skyward, and fancy decoration at the top, it is a perfect example of how architects of the day addressed the design challenges posed by the new penchant to reach for the heights. By the time it was built, both elevators and reinforced steel construction had been perfected.

The building in which the Stubbses live and spend much of their working day as dealers in old books, prints, and drawings was built in the prosperous years following the Civil War. From 1872 to 1895, their space belonged to Andrew Bogardus,

A section of the Turkish corner includes a nineteenth-century Indonesian group sculpture of three foreigners (a mustachioed British gent, a Hindu, and an African), a Newcomb pot (New Orleans Arts and Crafts), a piece of Rockingham china, and a Colosseum-inspired salad bowl by contemporary sculptor Tobias Mostel filled with a mélange of potpourri, a ceramic carpet ball, and a nineteenth-century figure of Venus.

a well-known photographer of the period. The wondrous new profession of photography was well suited to this fashionable area. Bogardus occupied the top floor, which at the time had a great skylight. He'd take photographic portraits against all manner of fancy or exotic backgrounds, such as dramatically draped curtains or Babylonian pillars. While renovating the loft, the Stubbses found several photographs he'd taken, including one of the famous midgets General Tom Thumb and his wife.

The studio was originally lit by gaslight, and all the fixture locations are still visible. During the renovation process, many layers of wallpaper were peeled away—some of them very garish, including a bright emerald green one with gold borders. By the changes in décor the Stubbses were able to approximate the dates when the various occupants lived there, rather like counting the rings of a tree trunk. Among other finds were two 1906 Indian-

head pennies used to jam a window shut.

In 1913 the building was given a limestone veneer, which fortunately did not impede its wonderful natural light, superb ventilation, and grand view. It is, John Stubbs says, "a much better building to look *from* than *at.*" There was once an elevator in one corner of the apartment but it is now out of service. The Stubbses hope to make it a fireplace someday. At the other end of their sixty-three-foot triangular floor plan was a dumbwaiter. The loft as presently designed is reminiscent of old European apartments in Paris or Rome, where the quirks of the past have to be accommodated. This often forces the imagination to work overtime. An associate in charge of restoration projects for Beyer, Blinder & Belle Architects and Planners, John is well qualified to apply technical know-how to his own imagination. Among other assignments, he has been involved with the restoration of Ellis Island, the

A late-nineteenth-century Neapolitan print of Vesuvius dominates the bookcase in the main gallery area. Drawings of sword handles are by a French jeweler. A head of Frank Lloyd Wright perches atop the bookcase. On the table is a nineteenth-century tabletop made of samples of Italian marble. The revolving bookstand in the foreground holds a late Regency cup; American art pottery by George Ohr of Biloxi, Mississippi; an 1850s Liverpool Transfer mug; Wiener Werkstätte glasses; and, lying down, a paper Japanese lady with a removable kimono, possibly a delicate way to indicate ailments to her physician. The racing cup was given to Jane Stubbs's great-great-grandfather, Keene Richards, who bred the winning horse, Limestone, in Kentucky.

New York Yacht Club, and most recently Grand Central Terminal.

Both Jane and John are from the South. He is from Monroe, Louisiana, and she from Natchez, Mississippi, about ninety miles east. They both grew up in bookish, antique-collecting families. After completing his architectural studies, John went to Italy and Egypt as an illustrator for archaeological excavations, and there he got hooked on the subject of ancient architecture and antiquities. Jane acquired her love of old objects through literature and the antebellum legacy of Natchez. Though they had met casually once or twice in the South, they were properly introduced at tea in New York's Waldorf-Astoria Hotel, where they discovered they were distant cousins and shared similar interests and a sense of humor. In addition to their Ladies' Mile space they own a gallery on the Upper East Side, at 835 Madison Avenue, which Jane runs.

Visitors are always first greeted by the Stubbses' twin pug dogs, Boris and Edward. The loft is arranged in railroad style, with one main room leading through to the next. Near the entrance is a small bathroom followed by a small kitchen, with an open hatch put in by the Stubbses. The first and most lasting impression of the apartment, naturally, is of books and prints. Interspersed among them are collections of a personal kind that run from antiquities through endless bowls of potpourri to American twentieth-century Southern glass. The décor itself is arrestingly quirky: a terra-cotta-painted wall is an apt foil for classical architectural drawings; a "Turkish corner"—so fashionable at the end of the nineteenth century—takes advantage of the splendid view; and a raised sleeping alcove is hidden behind a classically inspired facade that contains high-tech file cabinets designed for outsize prints. Jane found an eighteenth-century drawing of this facade in Milan. The design was adapted to include steps leading to the platform bed; Serge Dupin, a Tarrytown cabinet-maker, built the facade and the antiqued finish was painted by Nels Christiansen. Planned for the central archway is a trompe l'oeil painting of an ox cart ambling down the Via Appia. Clothes closets are concealed behind folding wooden doors that were once doors of interior public telephone booths. Paintings ancient and modern are perched on shelves or clustered on walls. These range from much-sought-after early-nineteenth-century gouaches of volcanoes to an elaborately framed oil portrait of the pugs by a friend.

Ladies' Mile is one of the most recently designated historic districts in New York. It is comforting to know that from now on these splendid facades—unlike some of those that once graced nearby Union Square—cannot be brutalized.

The windows form a prow shape and have a glorious view of buildings steeped in architectural history. In keeping with the age of the building, the Stubbses installed a Sarah Bernhardt–style "Turkish corner," with Oriental carpets covering different levels. Peacock feathers fill a Spanish oil jar. Glass prism sculptural pieces are by New York artist Bob Russell. The 1950s chairs are Italian.

The Stubbses' "bedroom" is above a storage cabinet hidden behind a classical facade. Books are piled up along the parapet that conceals the bed. A drawing of a classical head by modernist designer Herbert Lippman, done when he was a student, is used as a gate to bar the Stubbses' dogs from climbing up the steps to the bed. Over the telephone-booth closet is a nineteenth-century bas-relief, and on top of the bookcase is a massive carved wood finial. Antique Greek heads share space on bookshelves with a framed piece of antique needlepoint. The molded tin ceiling is typical of old New York commercial buildings.

A 1934 English country sofa sits in front of a German cabinet with baroque panels and columns. Above is a group of Wedgwood basaltware. On a shelf below are antique Greek heads and some antique leather-bound books. On the right is an African box, used to hold cassette tapes; to the left, Staffordshire dogs and a nineteenth-century Pompeian vase. Telephone-booth folding doors lead to closet space. Flower paintings are by Virginian Betty Stokes di Robilant. The lion is English.

TRIBECA MINIMAL DUPLEX

Of the well-to-do colonists who established their country seats north of Wall Street, the most prominent was British admiral Sir Peter Warren, who, in 1733, acquired much of the Bossen Bouwerie—as Dutch governor van Twiller had named the area—turning it into a splendid estate. Nowadays we know it as Greenwich Village. Admiral Warren married into the De Lancey family, the largest landowners in the city of New York. His daughters also married well. Two became the wives of peers: One wed Baron Southampton and the other married the Earl of Abingdon, whose name is perpetuated in Abingdon Square, now a children's playground in the West Village. A third married Colonel Skinner, after whom a street was named until the Revolution, when, because he was a Tory, it was renamed Christopher Street. Warren Street, in the trendy area of TriBeCa, commemorates Sir Peter himself.

Short for "Triangle Below Canal Street," TriBeCa is a fairly recent name for a neighborhood that has come back to life in the past decade. Due in part to the new and visually dazzling Battery Park City complex nearby, TriBeCa has become a desirable neighborhood not only for pacesetting artists who came in search of inexpensive studio space, but also for Wall Streeters and traditional families.

Aware of TriBeCa's redevelopment, Michael Somers and Cheryl Huff Somers bought a duplex in a recently renovated industrial building on Warren Street. They were attracted more by the ample amount of affordable space than by the stylishly unconventional downtown ambience. At the time, both worked in midtown Manhattan; he as vice president of a brokerage firm and she at *Ms.* magazine.

The Somerses were the second family to live in the duplex after the building was converted to residential use. The previous owners had divided each loftlike floor into two levels and completed the kitchen and a bathroom on the entrance floor, but little else had been done. The Somerses soon realized that they would need professional architectural help to design the large space to their specific requirements. Through her boss at *Ms.*, Cheryl found out about the architectural design firm Hogben & Glover. She was impressed by their work and they were subsequently retained. The extensive renovation took more than nine months to complete and involved much work that does not show, such as the installation of central air conditioning and complex electrical wiring.

The architectural team was assisted by Hogben's wife, Mason Perkins, an artist and colorist. The Hogbens met while working in Michael Graves's architectural office. She selected the paint colors to emphasize the architectural elements of the duplex. Inspiration came from the green patina of some pleasingly oxidized iron shutters on the building seen through the apartment's living room windows. A large wall dividing the living room from the kitchen and hall has been painted a subtle pale blue green; the color alters with the changing light. Equally striking and unconventional are a peacock blue architectural block and a terra-cotta-colored pillar.

Both Michael and Cheryl had previously lived in small, cluttered apartments and were determined to pare down the excess. They didn't want an apartment that looked obviously decorated or filled with expensive objects bought to impress. Rather, they wanted the vision of the architecture to shine through on every level. The architects worked with

The gym includes wall bars as well as rowing, track, and various muscle-building machines. The bedroom is reached by wood-topped stairs. The bed can be seen through the simple metal banister.

them to fulfill this goal and even to realize a few fantasies, including a spa area devoted to sleeping, working out, and luxuriating in the bath.

The spa was built on the bottom floor. It is an area intended for privacy. Guests who wander down to the spa's bathroom—with its four dramatic, if only decorative, glass doors—are, rather unnervingly, in full view. The gym ceiling is double height, the bathroom ceiling normal height, and the bedroom area opposite is on a raised platform reached by a short staircase. Under the bedroom platform is a luxuriously generous walk-in closet. Next to the bathroom, a fifth glass door opens onto a corridor leading to the utilities room and electrical center. The staircase leading to the upper floor had been freestanding, but was filled in and given light oak rises and treads. Paint in subtle grays covers the Sheetrock walls, and three-toned industrial carpeting covers the floor.

The bathroom is sophisticated and sybaritic. Its mahogany-framed doors are echoed by mahogany trim, imparting an expensive, masculine look to the bathing complex, which includes bath, shower, basin, and sauna. White Carrara marble tiles cover the walls. These were bought inexpensively through a newspaper advertisement. Black book-matched marble (that is, laid in consecutive slabs to enhance the graining) is used on the floor as well as for the tub, shower, and basin surrounds. Gray Turkish towels are warmed on heated towel racks. The sauna was custom built. As both clients and architects wanted a rich, modern effect throughout the bathroom, and standard fittings lacked the desired look, all the faucets, towel racks, toilet-paper holders,

Of the five mahogany-framed glass doors in the spa, four open onto the bathroom. The fifth door leads to the utilities area. The industrial tweed carpeting picks up the dark maroon color of the doors, the lighter brown oak of the stair treads and risers, and the steel gray of the workout machines.

soap dishes, lighting devices, and even the shower curtain were especially designed and custom made. As architect Russell Glover says, "Architects will design *everything* if you give them the chance."

The bedroom area is comfortable but unadorned. Chic black-and-white-patterned linens cover a bed that has chrome reading lamps at the head and a television set at the foot. Pleated gray window shades hide the view of another nearby industrial building. An alcove holds books, magazines, and a table desk; an ottoman covered with beige cotton provides a seat.

Directly across from the bedroom area, and right above the bathroom, is a mezzanine floor. It forms a narrow corridor open on one side and is lit with a series of custom-made translucent, square-shaded lights. At the end of the corridor is a small office with a desk and handy shelves. A new staircase, veneered in checkerboard oak, leads from the mezzanine to the ground floor, which comprises the entrance hall, kitchen, bathroom, and a large living room. The Somerses wanted to be able to entertain large groups expansively and small groups intimately. Hogben & Glover skillfully created areas on this floor to meet both needs. The previously installed kitchen is equipped with a double Garland stove and grill, a double and a single sink, two KitchenAid dishwashers, and a stainless steel two-door, Sub-Zero refrigerator and freezer, all efficient for large parties—and a caterer's dream come true. Lighting fixtures on wall and ceiling are dome

shaped. The most up-to-date gadgets stand on counters and in cupboards—Krups juicer, Braun coffee maker, Waring blender, and Alessio coffee set. Mies van der Rohe chairs of black leather on chrome frames from Knoll sit at a round, blackish green marble breakfast table supported by an industrial steel pedestal.

Just beyond the kitchen is the formal dining area, which is part of the living room space. A huge black, marble-topped oval table—designed by Joseph D'Urso for Knoll—is used for seated dinner parties, or as a buffet table for large groups. The same Miesian leather and chrome chairs surround it.

The sloping skylight spanning the width of the living room already existed, but Hogben & Glover enlarged three windows to admit more light, especially needed on the ground floor of these closely packed together industrial buildings. As the architectural remodeling progressed, Cheryl asked the design firm of Robert Simon & Associates for advice on furnishings. Plans were drawn up and she was walked through the D & D (Design & Decoration) Building, where, in the Angelo Donghia showroom, she quickly discovered fabrics and furnishings that had the feeling she was after. She selected the maroon leather-covered sofa and chair and the velour-covered armchairs that now form a conversational area. This area is defined by a carpet designed as a painting on the floor by Mason Perkins and signed M.P. in one corner. A gilded table with bird footprints on the top stands on metal bird's

At the top of the stairs is one of the Somerses' few but favorite decorative things—a crocodile of gilded terra-cotta lying on a four-poster with candles at each corner. It came from the Clodagh, Ross & Williams gallery in the East Village.

A generous walk-in closet is fitted beneath the sleeping platform. The chest of drawers is from Conran's.

In the dining area, the huge black marble table, designed by Joseph D'Urso, is from Knoll. The blue-green architectural wall varies with the changing light. The leather-and-chrome chairs were designed by Mies van der Rohe.

In the living room, the maroon leather sofa and armchair and the velour-covered armchairs are all from Angelo Donghia. The custom-made area rug was designed by Mason Perkins. *(overleaf)*

legs. A chrome-and-glass side table by Eileen Gray, the Irish designer who worked in Paris in the 1930s, and a mahogany-and-lacquer smoking stand from France are true Art Deco pieces—the owners' concession to the past. Also from Donghia is a black lacquer console and postmodern mirror with a split pediment. The room is lit by high-tech track lighting on the ceiling, high-tech black wall sconces, and modern black standing lamps.

The black-tiled bathroom on this floor has a long counter with two basins and backed by a mirror. There is also a shower and black-tiled soaking tub. The floor inside and outside the bath is of black nonslippery slate. Above the entrance floor is the highest level of the duplex, a loftlike space that serves as a library and sitting room.

The novelty of this apartment is that almost everything in it is spanking new but acquired with precise thought. Intentionally, very little is revealed of the owners' otherwise eclectic way of life. One would never know, for instance, that they drive a vintage Bentley, open their second home in Sag Harbor to Fresh Air kids, and have two Shar-Pei dogs called Killer and Kong, or that Cheryl likes to paint furniture and train her horse. What is obvious is that, in their New York residence, they welcome today's mode.

WEST VILLAGE ONE-ROOMER

In the days of the early European settlers, Manhattan north of Wall Street consisted of rolling, open fields traversed by country lanes that followed old Indian trails. The area that became Greenwich Village grew up on the site of an earlier Indian village.

During the eighteenth and nineteenth centuries, the west side of the Village developed more slowly than the east side, largely because the land was rather swampy, crossed by channels of sluggish water. Gradually small houses began to line the streets and were occupied mainly by tradesmen and craftsmen—weavers, carters, butchers, sail makers, builders, and blacksmiths—whose commerce required proximity to the nearby Hudson River.

One early West Village thoroughfare is Jane Street. It is said that after his duel with Aaron Burr, the fatally wounded Alexander Hamilton was brought from Weehawken, New Jersey, to William Bayard's house on this street. The house originally belonged to a Mr. Jaynes, after whom the street is named, according to Henry Moscow's *The Street Book*. In a metropolis of big, impersonal apartment buildings, the uniqueness of the Village lies in its human-scale houses. To find Franklin Roosevelt Underwood's apartment one enters the door of a house on Jane Street, passes right through the house, out the other side, and across a minute courtyard. There, tucked away behind a door with leaded-glass lights, is the pocket handkerchief–sized apartment in which he lives. It is not an independent structure, but attached to the back of a building that faces 12th Street.

What purpose Underwood's space originally served is not clear. Some suggest a stable, a tannery, or a washhouse. It is known that it was converted into residential space around 1924.

Composer/singer/piano player Franklin Under-

wood has lived in this tiny, one-room apartment for nearly twenty years. He first visited New York in the 1950s and he realized, as many had before him, that this was where, at least in his chosen field—musical theater—everything was happening. He wanted to share in the lively art, music, poetry, and jazz scene then centered around the Village.

Underwood was brought up on the family farm in Gilman, Illinois. When he was a boy, his father opened first one restaurant and then several more. His mother was a striking, vivacious woman who played the piano and sang for the customers. Franklin was impressed—especially, he says, by her flamboyant honky-tonk quality—so he, too, started playing the piano, picking up most of his skill by ear. Before long he was entertaining diners, too.

The piano became his life. In college he studied music and composition. During his stint in the army at West Point, he orchestrated for two bands and played the piano.

He found his apartment on Jane Street in the usual Village way, by seeing an advertisement and getting there first. The place was in bad shape then and, he says with a smile, it still is! Some previous tenant or landlord had installed a sleeping loft with wood steps leading up to it and rudimentary unpainted wood shelves surrounding it. A large skylight lit the space. The apartment had an unconventional, funky, starving-artist's allure that appealed to Underwood.

Apart from moving in some furniture and arranging his personal—and, to some, outlandish—collections, Underwood has done little to change it. Though he uses the excuse that he isn't handy around the house, there is a more deep-seated belief that some things are best left unchanged. His one attempt at bona fide decorating was to buy cotton

On the piano—which takes up most of the room's space—is vintage sheet music, some of Underwood's own compositions, and family snapshots. By the wall is a table full of tiny pieces of black memorabilia.

127

flannel printed with wild game birds at Macy's and staple it onto an ugly plastered wall that had been erected by a previous owner to conceal some undivulged horror. Even so, he allowed great gaps to show between the seams of the cloth, and left the selvage edge visible. When, as occasionally happens, the skylight leaks, in true *Sous les toits de Paris* style, it produces streams of tar stalactites. He rather liked these black protuberances at first, but now breaks them off and complains to the landlord. Though he fantasizes a lot, and keeps stacks of *World of Interiors* and *Architectural Digest* magazines by his bed, his decorating is more consistently inspired by the Midwest. He loves the early *Women's Day* feel of the homes of his childhood, where artist-manqué houseowners endlessly turned obsolete artifacts into decorative objects. "Where I come from, they paint *saws* and hang them on the wall!" He adds, "I'd quite like to have one myself." In his own kitchen can be found a classic of this ilk—a pair of ice tongs used to hold paper towels.

His furnishings have appeared more by chance than by serious, fanatical hunting. Most—and there's not room for much—are odd pieces from his hometown, such as idiosyncratic beaded-and-turned wood chairs made in the 1930s, well-worn handmade family quilts, and embroidered cushions that look surprisingly, and decoratively, sub-folk arty. By the bed, an embroider-by-numbers picture has been framed. Brimmed and banded hats in the Frank Sinatra–*Tender Trap* mode hang from a stag's antlers. An engraving of a farm scene was purchased because Underwood loved the look of the horse. A braided rug was handmade by a friend and collaborator, the composer/singer Richard Rodney Bennett. A Route 66 road sign of song fame was

From the doorway can be seen two chairs with beaded wood arms and legs. They are upholstered in forties dime-store printed cotton and come from Illinois. A wooden black doll, given as a gift, sits on the piano. Against the wall covered with printed cotton flannel is a mirror made out of a horse's collar from the family barn. An aerial photograph of the Underwood family farm hangs above a black-memorabilia cartoon.

Underwood's collection of Royal Bayreuth pottery shares space on the exposed-brick wall with a wedding picture of his parents.

discovered in an Illinois barn near the last remaining portion of the renowned coast-to-coast highway. Driftwood houses were bought from an artist in St. Thomas on one of Underwood's many piano-playing seasons in the Caribbean.

The largest piece of furniture in the tiny space is Underwood's piano. Family photographs ornament the top of it: his mother, in one snap with dark hair and in another as a blonde; a tinted photograph of Franklin as a toddler in short pants and long ringlets; and a family group at the Philadelphia opening of his musical *Lovely Ladies, Kind Gentlemen*, which was based on *Teahouse of the August Moon.* Under the sleeping loft is a poster for this musical, which played in San Francisco and Los Angeles before coming to New York, where it ran for only nineteen performances—far too short a time to make any money, but too long to qualify for wall space in Joe Allen's restaurant, where only the posters of six-day flops are hung.

Like many New Yorkers, Underwood is not above finding furniture on the street, where, if the timing is right, one can come across great discoveries. The tall but narrow bookcase that fits perfectly behind the front door was found this way. Most recently, a forties biscuit tin with a handle was rescued and now embellishes a milk can used as a side table.

Underwood's collection of black memorabilia, mostly small figurines, began modestly, but is slowly growing as friends find and give him pieces. He also collects Royal Bayreuth pottery, which, he says, people either hate or love. He first saw this gaudy orange-and-green pottery of leaves, fruit, and shellfish at his godmother's. He liked the color it brought to her kitchen, and she gave him a piece every birthday.

The bathroom is no larger than those on airplanes but nowhere near as high-tech. The kitchen is not big enough to swing his cat, Pauline, around in.

The apartment seems eminently suited to Franklin Underwood's life. He plays gentle, tasteful jazz in bars around town, but sometimes, looking around at today's musical tastes, wonders if he is the keeper of the wrong flame. Not that he's ready to change anything about his style of living. . . .

This overall shot of the apartment—from which a chair and side table had to be removed to make room for the tripod—gives an idea of just how tiny it is. The window under the sleeping loft looks into a bite-sized kitchen. The door to the left opens onto an equally diminutive bathroom. On the shelves surrounding the bed in the loft are driftwood houses. All the patchwork quilts, the embroidered cushion, and the two-handled pot belonged to Underwood's family.

FINE ART ON FIFTH

From 60th Street northward, Fifth Avenue is enhanced by Central Park, that grand "Greensward," as it was named by Frederick Law Olmsted and Calvert Vaux, the two men who conceived it. To be near grass and trees is a rare luxury in the concrete-and-glass maze of Manhattan. When Central Park was first designed in the mid-nineteenth century, the houses around it were mostly squatters' shacks. Now it is ringed dramatically with high-rise apartment blocks. Most were built in the 1920s and 1930s. Though smaller town houses line side streets, the apartment buildings overlooking the park—however varied in fabric and detail—present a huge wall of impersonal windows. They have grand lobbies with sheltering awnings to protect residents from the elements as they step from door to vehicle. With large windows, high ceilings, elaborate moldings, marble-floored halls, and back entrances for servants, apartments in this part of Manhattan are highly sought after. No wonder, then, that a publisher of fine books moved into one such Fifth Avenue apartment in 1986 when it came on the market. It offered the space he needed to display and enjoy his unique agglomeration of art objects and paintings, and contrasted nicely with his smaller apartment in Paris, where he also lives and works.

His Russian parents collected paintings, mostly Impressionist, some of which he inherited. Their home was decorated by the Parisian firm Jansen, and they lived a sophisticated, international life, the taste for which, along with their love of art, they passed on to their three sons. Paintings by Sisley, Pissarro, Renoir, and Degas from his parents' trove serve as a foil for the publisher's own remarkable accumulation of Old Master paintings and Renaissance bronzes. A student of art history, he became

interested in bronzes at a time, he says, when they were not nearly as expensive as they are today.

His interest is not limited to European art, however, but extends to many different cultures. In one room of his New York apartment—indeed, on one library secretaire—can be found antique pieces from Mexico, Africa, Easter Island, New Guinea, and India; in the entrance hall a twelfth-century Thai prosperity god sits in front of an eighteenth-century Swedish painting.

To assemble these disparate (yet, because of his consistent eye, quite compatible) *objets d'art*, he called upon a friend, Pierre Scapula, who, like him, lives in both New York and Paris, to help with the often exciting and sometimes agonizing decisions about décor. The apartment has a distinctly European air, a grand one at that, due to the selection of luxurious Parisian fabrics used for upholstery, curtains, and walls. There is a keen intellectual edge to the grandeur.

The tone is set in the entrance hall, which retains its original black-and-white marble floor and crown molding. The walls have been painted to resemble blocks of warm, ocher-tinged stone, and the doors are painted dark faux bois. Centered in the room is a claw-footed Swedish Empire plinth bearing a delicately modeled terra-cotta figure of a slender and youthful St. George standing over a vanquished—and rather small—dragon, circa 1520. According to Sir John Pope-Hennessy, it is by the Master of the St. John and St. David Statuettes. A bucolic French terra-cotta straw-hatted figure holding a goblet stands against one wall. Against another are two marble-topped Italian tables; above them hangs a seventeenth-century still life by the Dutch master Melchior d'Hondecoeter. It shows a hunter's pouch and his catch of the day, including two

On the silk-damask-upholstered walls of the library is a portrait of the owner's mother painted in 1948 by Salvador Dali. An antique paisley shawl drapes the sofa.

Centered in the entrance hall is a terra-cotta St. George on a claw-footed plinth. On the wall to the right is a still life by Evaristo Baschenis. Pictures on either side of the door leading to the dining room are, on the right, a rustic scene by Peter Angelisz and, on the left, a still life by Melchior d'Hondecoeter. In the foreground is a French eighteenth-century terra-cotta figure.

rabbits. Another brilliantly painted still life by Bergamese artist Evaristo Baschenis depicts a mandolin, a violin, other musical instruments, and a globe beneath a gold-fringed draped curtain. An eighteenth-century rustic scene of apple sellers is by Anglo-Dutch painter Peter Angelisz. Like beautiful women at an elegant party, every painting in the hall attracts the eye yet is complemented by its companions.

Leading off the hall through mirrored doors is the large drawing room. Its opulent ambience stems from the spectacular Savonnerie carpet, one of seventeen made for Versailles. Sponged pale peach walls are skirted with marbleized trim; upholstery and curtains are of heavy auburn-and-amber silk damask from the Parisian firm Braquenié. Furniture is eighteenth-century French with flourishes of fine marquetry, gilt bronze, and ormolu. A Chinese coromandel screen decorates most of one wall.

Coffee tables are of Chinese lacquered wood, protected by clear glass. Precious and remarkable objects include a pair of Chinese Foo dogs (believed to be twelfth-century) glazed with textured spots. They flank a gilt-bronze-and-ormolu clock decorated with white Vincennes porcelain roses and Chinese roosters. These pieces sit on a marquetry table by Roussel; above is Boucher's *Allegory of Autumn*. A French eighteenth-century mantel displays ormolu-and-blue Sèvres vases and gilt candlesticks. Above the mantel is a large gilt-bronze clock depicting the New World; it is set on a mirror flanked by Chinese porcelain birds on French Regency brackets. In the center of the room is a French eighteenth-century mechanical table on which stands a gilt-bronze late-sixteenth-century Sienese figure of a saint. By a window is a Venetian landscape by Antonio Diziani. At the other end of the room, two beautiful small Monnoyer paintings of lilies and roses hang near a landscape by the seventeenth-century French artist Antoine Pierre Patel.

The drawing room leads into the dining room, where the atmosphere is Tolstoyan French Empire with a dash of twentieth-century fantasy thrown in. A Fabergé samovar rests on the sideboard. A large bookcase lines one wall, and on either side of it are costume designs by Sudeikin for one of Diaghilev's productions of *Petrushka* for the Ballets Russes. A grand piano—which the owner plays—sits by a window covered in Austrian shades trimmed with fleur-de-lis and bird-patterned braid. On the piano, when its lid is shut, is a seventeenth-century bronze copy of a Flavian head of a Roman matron. Columns flanking the piano hold stylish alabaster urns from Jansen that conceal lights. For dinner parties, real candles are lit on French Empire wall sconces. Around the Empire table are two different sets of upholstered, slope-armed, oval-backed chairs that have a 1930s' smartness, although they date from a century earlier. The table is set with a pink cloth and matching initialed napery that impart a rosy glow to guests. By each of the gold-and-turquoise-bordered eighteenth-century Sèvres plates from Nelson A. Rockefeller's estate are a trio of tall-stemmed, gold-embellished wineglasses. A Renaissance bronze lion and tiger crouch on the table as decoration. For musical evenings, the dining room furniture is moved, doors to the drawing room and hall are thrown open, and chairs are set up for as many as a hundred guests.

Perhaps the most interesting room of all is the library. With walls upholstered in Empire red-and-gold silk damask, this room imparts a traditional European air, filled as it is almost to overflowing with French Empire furniture set on a vivid Oriental-motif, modern wall-to-wall carpet by Braquenié. Yolk yellow striped *gaufrage* (French steam-pressed velvet) covers French Empire chairs. On the marble mantelpiece two marble obelisks flank a Roman seventeenth-century crucifix by Guglielmo della Porta.

On a round French Empire table topped with scagliola, small Renaissance black-patinated bronzes, including a ram's head, satyrs, and sea dragons, surround a carved rhinoceros horn goblet depicting hunting scenes from the New World. On top of a working desk, gilt bronzes share company with antique Greek icons and a pearl-trimmed twelfth-century Kievan reliquary. Renaissance bronzes also adorn a pair of demi-lune English Regency side tables, and on a marble-topped French Empire commode, fifteenth- and sixteenth-century bronzes from Padua and Venice stand beneath a Degas painting of dancers. The most arresting painting in the room is a portrait of the owner's mother in a surreal landscape, painted in 1948 by Salvador Dali.

Off the library is a small bathroom that the owner has transformed from a banal, pale green tiled room into an urbane powder room simply by marbleizing the original tiles with deep crimson. Glossy black trim outlines the faux marble and a marble floor was installed.

A bar opens off the library. All but the floor in this miniroom is mirrored. Here, in a hidden closet, extra chairs are stored for musical soirées. The bar forms a passage to the owner's bedroom, where the walls are upholstered in striped cotton, with an elaborate looped Romantic border at the crown molding. The room is simple, lit by 1820 French Empire wall sconces, and tidy, thanks to ample walk-in closets. Over the bed, which has a headboard and spread covered in a Tree of Life design, is a Picasso print of his wife Jacqueline. A Jack Youngerman drawing hangs to one side.

As the owner admits, the bones of this Manhattan apartment were already there when he moved in. What he has created is a setting not only for his art objects but also for enjoying the art of conversation—an updated version of a drawing room in *War and Peace*, the sort of place where pivotal relationships begin over a table of antique snuffboxes. This apartment manages to combine the best of the Old and New worlds.

Upholstered chairs from the 1830s surround an Empire dining table. On the piano is an Italian seventeenth-century copy of a Flavian head flanked by alabaster urns on columns from Jansen. The wallpaper border is an eighteenth-century documentary from Mauny. The Sèvres plates came from the Nelson Rockefeller estate.

Displayed on this secretaire are an Olmec head, a New Guinea wooden spirit, a Mexican figure from the pre-classic period, a Hellenistic head, an Indian bronze, and an African carving.

A fancifully inlaid scagliola table on a French Empire base holds a circle of Renaissance bronzes. In the center is a seventeenth-century goblet from Augsburg carved from a rhinoceros horn.

HUDSON RIVER HOUSEBOAT

One of New York's truly private neighborhoods can be found at the 79th Street Boat Basin right on the Hudson River. This community of houseboats is visible only to motorists driving along the West Side Highway or to joggers running along the footpath at the edge of the river. Yachts and houseboats bob in the water, moored to rows of continually shifting wood-planked piers. The Boat Basin is not accessible to the general public; a strong metal fence prevents anyone from casually entering the dock area without a key.

Among the owners of the hundred or so boats permanently berthed here, an unusually tight-knit feeling has evolved. Boat owners look out for their neighbors because, more than elsewhere, their homes are at the mercy of the elements. Ever present is the threat of sinking, becoming adrift, or sudden fire.

The 79th Street Boat Basin was created by the influential Robert Wagner when he was Commissioner for Public Works in the late 1930s and early 1940s. It is maintained by the city's Parks and Recreation Administration. A dock house is in charge of day-to-day maintenance; its window displays current charges for renting space and for hookups to the water lines and electrical cables placed at intervals along the docks.

Simone di Bagno is an Italian who has lived here since 1977. He came to America in 1975 when he was offered a job as a filmmaker for the United Nations. If he were unable to live on his boat, he says, he would no longer want to live in New York. Here, he maintains, he has fresh air, a fabulous, indestructible view, and sympathetic if unorthodox neighbors. The slightly raffish life-style suits him, as it does most of those who share his surroundings.

Di Bagno was born in Rome, where he started his career as a photographer and journalist. In the 1960s he and some friends spent a year in India, traveling all over the subcontinent by car. On this trip he discovered that his forte was making documentary films. Back in Rome, he began working his way up in the movie business, including a stint as an assistant to Fellini, until the United Nations job brought him to New York. It wasn't long before he found out about the 79th Street Boat Basin and fell in love with it, its community spirit in particular.

At first di Bagno rented a boat, but eventually he bought the *Excalibur*, which was made of wood. Unfortunately, he found it had a recurring tendency to sink—twice a year, on the average! He was forced to keep on replacing his décor, and for this reason he could keep nothing really precious on the vessel. His present boat is unnamed. He chose this rather nondescript Chris Craft Aqua Home for its fiberglass hull, which renders it unsinkable. The craft was discovered in a small marina in Westport, Connecticut, where it had been used, sold, gutted, somewhat fixed up as a floating workshop, then more or less given up. Not only his friends, but the Boat Basin's maintenance man, Israeli boat carpenter Doron Katzman, as well, advised di Bagno against buying the engineless, dilapidated Chris Craft, but di Bagno was determined. He arranged for Katzman to tow it all the way from Westport, and together they worked out plans to convert the boat into a remarkable residence.

They both realized the boat would need a lot of work and that the available space had to be used to advantage. To the right of the entrance to the main cabin, a banquette was given a large retractable seat that can double as a guest bed. Underneath it are storage units. The area that once housed the

Houseboats of many varieties are moored to walkways that have electrical and water hookups at intervals.

engine was made into an unusually generous state-room for this type of boat—most houseboats are equipped with space-saving bunk beds. To increase the illusion of space, di Bagno set out to find reflecting glass. He rummaged through furniture on sale at the Salvation Army and came upon large, flamboyantly carved, wood-framed mirrors. To create an amusing if eccentric contrast to the untreated plywood walls and built-in plywood units, di Bagno himself gilded and antiqued most of the mirror frames. In the stateroom alone, twelve mirrors line the walls, and four others are found in the main cabin. Taking the gilded-frame motif to the point of surrealism, di Bagno placed a frame around the screen of his television set, then added gold bullion-fringed epaulets from a Roman carabiniere uniform to the upper corners.

Other space-saving devices include built-in drawers under the large bed, a built-in clothes closet, a stack of drawers for sweaters—which also serves as a table for his computer—and bookshelves, both in the stateroom and main cabin. All these carpentry details were constructed and installed by Katzman.

Lighting throughout the boat has been de-signed in a whimsical manner. Di Bagno noted the tendency of New Yorkers to leave their Christmas illuminations in situ long after the holiday season has passed. He was impressed with the fairy lights decorating the trees all year round at Central Park's Tavern on the Green restaurant. In his dark and windowless state room, di Bagno outlined all his gilded mirrors with Christmas tree lights, which use minimal amounts of electricity. He also wound them up the two classical columns—found in a salvage

The bed in the large stateroom is flanked by floor-to-ceiling pillars bought for five dollars each and painted by di Bagno. Two truncated fiberglass columns from Canal Street serve as bedside tables. Twelve Salvation Army mirrors, most of them gilded by di Bagno, add space to the room. Christmas tree lights add festivity.

trading center—flanking his double bed. For additional light, he can switch on green glass–shaded reading lamps that sit on truncated fiberglass columns used as bedside tables.

In the main cabin, during the day, the problem is often too much light. Here windows have been hung with waterproof blinds fashioned from cut-down shower curtains. Appropriately for a world traveler, these are printed with a map of the earth.

Loose furniture throughout the boat is expendable and almost all Salvation Army. An over-scale rattan sofa equipped with a massive beanbag of a cushion sits in one corner. The cushion can be moved out onto the prow or a roof deck for sunning. Large square pillows covered in white and off-white fabrics of varying textures can be used indoors or out, for they cannot fade in the sun. Indonesian batiks cover cushions used inside. The Third World is well represented by many of the objects that decorate the interior: An Indian painting on silk, an Indonesian embroidered hanging, an embroidered felt hat from the Golden Triangle, an American hard hat embellished by Asian artisans, a carved-wood owl, an Ivory Coast wicker cabinet—all these were given to di Bagno or were gleaned by him while filming on location. Objects found closer to home include a stained-glass window, two Sergeant Pepperish uniforms, an elegant Dior *mouchoir* held in an articulated wooden mannequin's

hand—found in a trash can and under consideration as a Cocteauesque door handle—and some cheerful lapses of taste such as gaudy roller skates.

Perhaps most striking of all is di Bagno's dining room. Permanently fixed to the roof directly above the main cabin is a regular dining room table. It is covered with a white plastic tablecloth and, in a fanciful nod to formality, two candelabra—with candles—are securely nailed into it! Surrounding it is a matching set of Salvation Army chairs that can be turned on their sides and tucked beneath the table when not in use.

The head—the nautical term for a bathroom—is small but appears larger because of flexible, mirrored plastic on the wall beside the toilet. Pasted on the plastic are explicit instructions explaining how to deal with boat plumbing, which, due to lack of water pressure, is unlike most plumbing on land. The diminutive washbasin is concocted from a copper salad bowl set into waterproofed plywood. Three plywood steps lead up to a shower. Because rough waves following in the wake of large vessels can topple objects, shelves are given safety rails of nailed-on rope. Lighting in the head consists of plastic tubing containing tiny bulbs. This form of lighting is commonly used to edge dark steps in cinemas and theaters. Di Bagno looped his around mirror and ceiling. To save space, a sliding door of Brazilian wood screens the head.

The head was installed by Doron Katzman following di Bagno's design. The tiny washbasin is a copper salad bowl found at Zabar's, the West Side gourmet emporium. The brown rattan cabinet came from Africa's Ivory Coast. Theater strip lighting was found in Texas.

A galley installed by boat carpenter Doron Katzman doubles as a bar. The Indian painting on silk and rice paper is from Rajasthan and depicts the story of Krishna. A wooden owl by the sink was a present to di Bagno from some Indonesian women when he made a film in Indonesia on women's rights.

In the main cabin the retractable corner banquette was constructed over the boat's original banquette, increasing seating space on top and storage space beneath. The steering wheel is now merely decorative, because the boat's engine has been removed. The silver-and-black helmet was crafted by Indonesians from an American hard hat. A Thai Buddha sits on the gilded television set. The ON AIR sign is a relic from a 1940s radio station. A lavishly embroidered Indonesian hanging is quaintly lit by a picture lamp.

For stylish alfresco dining, Di Bagno nailed a table complete with candelabra to the roof of the main cabin. Surrounding it are Salvation Army chairs.

Opposite the head is the galley, a tiny space containing a sink, some shelves, a hot plate, a portable oven, and a waist-high refrigerator. The wood counter has been treated with a waterproof finish. A hinged shelf masks the galley if need be. This shelf serves as a bar and is within easy reach of the main cabin. Electric wall units provide enough heating to make the boat cozy during the winter months.

Three steps between the main cabin and stateroom are lit by more Christmas tree lights. Beside them the plywood wall is hung with framed awards, certificates, and medals won by di Bagno

for his domumentary films. Titles include *Footnotes to a War*, *Galápagos*, *My Special Land*, *The Delicate Giant*, and *Shelter for the Homeless*.

Like many New York neighborhoods, the 79th Street Boat Basin has its own local association that promotes community events and celebrations. Visitors are struck by the variety of sizes, shapes, and styles of houseboats. Some have roof gardens riotous with flowers and vegetables. Pets and bicycles can be found on many decks, and one boat has a regular front door! The effect is rare in New York—a delightful and decorative stage-set shantytown with Club Med overtones.

BIEDERMEIER IN BROOKLYN HEIGHTS

Angus Wilkie is one of those rarities, a true New Yorker, raised on 62nd Street in Manhattan. He now lives in Brooklyn Heights, however, that "grande dame of Brownstone Brooklyn," to quote from David W. McCullough's *Brooklyn . . . And How It Got That Way*. This half-mile-long bluff faces a captivating view of the southern tip of Manhattan with its ever-soaring office buildings. The Heights were established as a suburb for lawyers, stockbrokers, and shipping magnates who made their fortunes in lower Manhattan, and it has often been said that those who live in Brooklyn Heights need know nothing about the rest of Brooklyn.

When Brooklyn, one of New York City's five boroughs, was first settled by the Dutch in 1636, it was inhabited by the Carnarsees, a branch of the matriarchally organized Lenni-Lenape Indians, who called it the Sandy Place. The Dutch named it Breuckelen, or "broken land" (some translate it as "marsh land"), and this name, anglicized, is still in use today.

Brooklyn Heights has "tree-shaded streets and bluestone paved sidewalks lined by rows of fine old brick and brownstone houses behind decorative iron fences, and distinguished churches in the romantic styles, dating back to when this was the most easily accessible, desirable, and aristocratic suburb of New York." This is from Clay Lancaster's *Old Brooklyn Heights*, written in 1960.

Because of its commanding view, the Heights became a strategic site for the colonists during the Revolutionary War. Its era as a residential suburb— New York City's first bedroom community—began in 1814 with the establishment of steam ferry service between Manhattan and Brooklyn. According to Lancaster, at that time a number of land-

owners—whose names live on in such streets as Middagh, Pierrepont (originally Pierpont, but frenchified by Henry Pierrepont, son of Brooklyn Heights' real estate promoter Hezekiah Pierpont), Hicks, Remsen, and Joralemon—began dividing their respective holdings into 25-by-100-foot building lots. Churches were built on many of these lots during the piously respectable nineteenth century—when Henry Ward Beecher filled three thousand seats every Sunday at the New Plymouth Church—and to this day the area is heavy with religious organizations of every denomination.

Remsen Street was opened in 1825 by Henry Remsen, who lived in the area that became Grace Court. In 1839, in the middle of the building boom that lasted from the 1820s until the Civil War, three connected houses were constructed on Remsen Street in the prevailing Federal style. The one in which Angus Wilkie lives was first owned by Henry K. Brown, a physician. In those days the house had a front stoop and a lowered entrance, and there were stone hoods over the windows.

The house was "modernized" around the 1880s: An addition was made to the back and a mansard roof was built on top, creating a full new floor. Victorian moldings and wood-and-marble fireplaces updated the interior. On the second floor a pier glass typical of the late nineteenth century but rarely found today was installed and is still in place. The iron railing now in front of the building dates from this time as well.

Mr. Wilkie's apartment—which he shares with a large, very furry dog—straddles the two building eras; the present entrance, kitchen, living room, and bathroom are part of the 1880s addition, while the bedroom belongs to the original 1839 structure. Of course the bathroom and kitchen did not exist as

This Brooklyn Heights Federal style house, built in 1839, was given a mansard roof in the 1880s.

A cluster of favorite things ornaments the Biedermeier secretary in the living room. Polished Russian burlwood boxes, wooden balls, Bluejohn—a unique stone found in Derbyshire, England—and Italian marble rulers are all artifacts made in the eighteenth or nineteenth centuries.

A suite of cherrywood-veneer furniture with ebony inlay and elegant curved legs stands by the window in the living room. Made by top Viennese cabinetmaker Josef Danhauser in 1835, it was intended to be an ensemble—an early dinette set! The tilt-top table with its subtle beveled edge stands firmly on three masculine columns. To the left, an architectural drawing of a column echoes the wood column-shaped cupboard below.

such during the nineteenth century, but were converted to their present use in the twentieth century.

All of Brooklyn Heights is now designated a historic district, prohibiting any architectural changes to the exteriors of these early brownstones. Even without this stipulation, the present owners of the building, architect Edward Knowles and his wife, Barbara, actively maintain the historic integrity as well as the practical efficiency of the house. Recently they had the copper sheeting replaced and the outside cornice painstakingly restored. Their daughter Mary lives in the house and watches over it like a super superintendent.

After studying literature at Yale, Angus Wilkie tried out the financial world at Salomon Brothers. Three years later he switched to teaching eighth

On the living room mantel are pleasingly decayed nineteenth-century Viennese tin jars. Paintings on the wall are by Isidore Pils, August Frederick Behrens, and Leonid Osipovich Pasternak (father of author Boris). A Viennese daybed, covered in Fortuny cotton damask, is flanked by 1820 walnut tables, all Viennese Biedermeier. On the tables are bronze French Empire *objets*. The German Biedermeier book cupboard of walnut veneer with tiger-birch inlay is topped by 1770 English Delft. The two Wiener Werkstätte chairs on either side of the fireplace are Wilkie's earliest furniture purchase.

graders at St. Bernard's School, a job he found far more fulfilling if less lucrative. Despite diminished financial returns, in the process of furnishing his apartment he could not resist buying an expensive pair of chairs made in 1914 by Wiener Werkstätte designer Josef Hoffmann. A little later he discovered Biedermeier furniture, which, as he describes it, "spoke" to him. In 1981 he bought his first Biedermeier piece—a small mirror that now hangs in his hallway—from the Niall Smith antiques shop.

The transition from Josef Hoffmann to Biedermeier was not out of character. Wilkie was to discover that the Viennese designer was one of the first champions of the earlier bourgeois style, and Hoffmann's enthusiasm led to the recognition of Biedermeier as a bona fide style. Hoffmann's own work shared the same properties of simplicity, geometry, and attention to function combined with elegance.

The name *Biedermeier* does not refer to a cabinetmaker of the period but is a play on words, combining *bieder*, meaning plain or unpretentious, and *Meier*, a common German surname. To begin with it was a denigrating term (somewhat parallel to "kitsch"), often used in comic verse to mock burgher piety. It was not applied to furnishings until the late nineteenth century, and then it was used

disparagingly. The style was neglected by academics and art historians for nearly a century, and to this day it is frequently criticized by English and French dealers in the world of interiors. To contemporary eyes, the furniture, when it is good—and not all of it is—looks remarkably good, and blends well with many other kinds of furniture.

Once bitten by the Biedermeier bug, Angus Wilkie rallied his scholar's background and searched for information. His research led him to Germany and Austria, where Biedermeier flourished during the postwar years of 1815 to 1848. "It was a style," he says, "which owed a significant debt to French Empire and English Regency designs; however, its form was a pared-down version of these antecedents. After the Napoleonic wars Biedermeier furniture emerged as a simple statement in comparison to the opulence of Empire. It was made by local cabinetmakers for the prosperous bourgeoisie evolving throughout Germany and the Austrian Empire." For this reason, very few pieces are either signed or dated, though the Biedermeier style passed through various phases, so dates or places of origin—Austria, Germany, or fringe countries such as Sweden—can usually be determined.

Wilkie became so enthralled by what he describes as the last flowering of pre-industrial design

that he learned German in order to study the most comprehensive books on the subject. Eventually he wrote his own book, *Biedermeier*, which was published in 1987. He lectures on nineteenth-century furniture and decorative arts. For a couple of years he dealt in the furniture and owned a shop on Grand Street in Manhattan. Now, however, his interest lies in writing fiction.

Biedermeier objects and paintings dot his small but uncluttered apartment. But all Biedermeier and nothing else is not completely satisfactory to our more eclectic eyes, so the rooms have been tempered with seemly pieces of other styles that are not out of character. French Empire bronze candlesticks and artifacts adorn side tables, and each has been chosen precisely for its intellectual appeal, amusing anecdote, or historic reference, as well as for decorative content. Dark gray green pleated shades (designed by Wilkie) enhance each lamp. Collections of burlwood boxes, marble rulers, and Derbyshire Bluejohn catch the eye. On the plain painted walls hang eighteenth- and nineteenth-century architectural drawings, suspended on fine wires that themselves form subtle geometric patterns. And everywhere there are columns, both as objects and drawings.

"I suppose I have safe taste," admits Wilkie of his pictures and pieces, knowing full well that none of them, in this Brooklyn Heights setting, can be faulted.

In the bedroom, a TV set is sandwiched between a Biedermeier collar box above and an 1820s tambour chest below. The wall is decorated with eighteenth- and nineteenth-century drawings. Over the bed is a landscape by Danish painter Carl Vilhelm Balsgaard (1812–1893).

Wilkie contributed the brass fixtures but otherwise the bathroom is much as it was when installed between the world wars. He added a black-and-white shower curtain, a Napoleonic metal campaign chair, and an English tole hatbox under the sink to hold soaps and toiletries. Horn mugs crown the medicine cabinet and an antique sword hangs beside it.

MIDTOWN ACCUMULATION

Behind the impressive New York Public Library, in the center of the towering buildings and teeming traffic of mid-town Manhattan, is a block of greens-ward called Bryant Park. The park has served various functions over the years. In the 1820s it was a potter's field. In 1853 it was host to the Crystal Palace, which housed the New York Exhibition of that year. Five years later the building was destroyed by fire. During the Civil War troops used the spot as a drilling and camping ground. In the latter part of the nineteenth century the land adjoined the Croton Reservoir and the park was known as Reservoir Square. In 1884 its name was changed to Bryant Park in honor of abolitionist William Cullen Bryant. The reservoir itself was filled in during the late 1890s and the public library took its place.

Buildings grew up around the green space. One of them, the Engineers' Building, was erected by Andrew Carnegie in 1907 as a club for those in the engineering profession. The building boasted a grand staircase, an impressive dining room and ballroom, and, on the higher floors, bedrooms for members to stay in when visiting New York. The club eventually spread over four buildings. The complex was altered when the buildings were bought and turned into co-op apartments between 1978 and 1979.

The new landlords divided the high-ceilinged rooms, transforming some into duplexes, adding stairs and sleeping balconies. The results in many cases are strangely shaped, long, narrow rooms, but all of them have a great deal more character than the usual bland shoe boxes of most New York apartments.

Part of the building's charm is the spacious lobby, with its Oriental carpet, elaborate marble staircase, and grand hallways, big enough to throw splendid parties—with the neighbors' cooperation. Many of the rooms have retained their deeply molded plaster ceilings, elaborate crown moldings, overscale fireplaces, and Honduran mahogany woodwork.

Sheila Shwartz, a designer, was one of the first to move in after the renovation took place. She was joined by her husband, Irving, a printing executive. Since then she has been elected president of the co-op board.

Sheila Shwartz started an antiques and collectibles firm called Faces of Time. The original concept of adapting antique watch faces has since stretched into many other areas. Now Faces of Time supplies antique accessories to stores and showrooms throughout the country, with the Ralph Lauren shops being her biggest and best-known customer. The New York specialty store Henri Bendel has just opened Sheila's first Faces of Time atelier. It is to Sheila that the stylists and designers turn when they need a display of authentic theme articles to enhance luxurious or sporty merchandise. Sheila also designs and manufactures a range of goods such as magnifying glasses with antique handles, many from old canes or umbrellas, or cuddly yet refined one-of-a-kind teddy bears equipped with antique accessories. The apartment has become a wonderfully cluttered rabbit warren evoking childhood memories—or what one would like to think might have been childhood memories if only one had been born in an earlier time!

Sheila was dissatisfied with the rather puny stair rails installed when the building was converted into apartments. She designed and had installed mahogany banisters of a more robust nature. The staircase leads to a narrow balcony floor with a full bathroom. Though many other owners use the

In the foreground of the living room are antique dolls, a swan decoy, a trunk filled with magnifying glasses with antique handles, a tin boat (part of a collection), antique suitcases, fishing rods, wooden bowling balls, athletes' discuses, and needlepoint cushions. On shelves by the stairs is an array of paired candlesticks.

upper floor as a bedroom, Sheila has built in a wall of glass-fronted closets, and prefers to use a convertible bed downstairs. The apartment possesses an unusually large fireplace—which would have made sense when the room was twice as big—with a front of malachite-looking green marble. It makes a perfect shelf to display decorative objects. A small but workable kitchen, a powder room, a walk-in closet, and an office/workroom with enough space for a large desk, a cupboard, and two chairs complete the layout. Meals are eaten at a table by the window that overlooks Bryant Park.

Sheila is an inveterate collector and her habitat teems with ever-changing décor. One day a group of deliciously worn leather saddles might be piled over the sofa with a stack of paisley shawls draped on top. China-headed dolls on miniature wicker chairs or in beds with lacy covers, bunches of extraordinary walking sticks, old globes of the world, silver hairbrushes, Victorian tartan boxes, vintage sports items, linen pillow cases, shagreen leather cases, necklaces, glitter globs, gravy boats, and hat stands are all mixed up in an array so fantastical that the eye is never bored. Objects move in and out continually, some for business, most for pleasure. Given the ferreting, acquisitive skill of the owner, this apartment will always be a place of wonder.

Inside the entrance one is greeted by a variety of antique hats.

An intimate supper can be enjoyed at one end of the knowingly cluttered living room. Lusterware plates, coffee cups, and saucers look well against the antique paisley shawl used as a tablecloth. The mélange of objects inlcudes a bead-draped antique tailor's dummy, a child's sailboat, an old radio sitting on a glass case full of shagreen boxes, botanical prints, dolls, and antique silver.

A sofa converts into a double bed, which is made up with an antique white lace coverlet and lace-edged pillows. Nearby is a massive green marble fireplace. Reflected in the overmantel mirror is the upstairs balcony. Ivory objects—created long before the ban on ivory—are displayed on the mantelpiece.

Never content with just one of anything, the owner has amassed a number of old-fashioned golf clubs. She is now involved with supplying the Ralph Lauren Golf Shops with their antique accessories.

PARK AVENUE PENTHOUSE

Penthouses are part of Manhattan's folklore. As Rodgers and Hart wrote: "See the pretty penthouse, top of the roof/The higher up the higher the rent goes." A penthouse with a verdant terrace is the ultimate in New York glamour.

Just before the crash of 1929, New York's most luxurious apartment buildings were rising faster and higher than ever before. Fifth and Park avenues on the Upper East Side were the streets of choice. A pioneer New York retailer who was also a builder, Jesse Isadore Strauss, knew firsthand what it was like to live in the grand style—he resided in one of his own buildings, which was designed by Rosario Candela. Strauss also built the adjoining building, the penthouse of which is now owned by textile executive Eldo Netto and his family.

The Nettos are the second family to occupy the duplex penthouse since it was built. The previous occupant was Charles T. Wilson and his family. After Mr. Wilson's death some years ago, his widow continued to live in the duplex until her recent death. The apartment, which boasts windows with views in all four directions, proved irresistible to the new tenants.

After a career of some twelve years in international banking, Netto invested in a small textile operation together with a friend from university days, Alan Campbell. Shortly thereafter, he bought venerable and staid Cowtan & Tout, a company that originated in the early 1920s when, at the behest of the J. P. Morgan family, a branch of the London firm Cowtan & Sons was established in New York especially to decorate and furnish the Morgan yacht and various houses. After enjoying a period of growth and expansion in the 1920s and '30s, the firm grew increasingly specialized under

the idiosyncratic but charmingly doddery leadership of Rose Tout (widow of the founder's son) and Rose's sister, Eve. By the time Netto discovered Cowtan & Tout it had become a well-kept secret as a purveyor of hand-blocked chintzes and wallpapers to those relatively few architects and designers interested in working with documentary designs.

Netto's acquisition of the company coincided with the booming English country house style of the late 1970s. The business grew rapidly. It is now one of the decorating industry's major suppliers of wallpapers and fabrics and its recent merger with the prestigious English firm Colefax & Fowler has further enhanced its importance and influence.

The Nettos' penthouse has its own spacious elevator hall. To one side of the entrance gallery is the drawing room, which has two pairs of glass-paneled doors facing east and opening onto a balcony, and two large windows facing west toward Central Park. The dining room, oak-paneled library, large kitchen, and butler's pantry with adjoining rooms for staff are also on the lower floor, as is the master bedroom suite, with its own private terrace facing north and east. A newly installed forged-steel balustrade, painted midnight blue and highlighted by gilt ornamentation and a polished brass rail, ascends to the second floor, where there are two family bedrooms and baths, and a study. The entire upper floor is surrounded by a planted terrace providing wide views east and west.

Though the original layout remains essentially unchanged, the replacement and updating of electrical wiring and plumbing was unavoidable, as was the total renovation of the kitchen. The decision to replace the whole staircase provided an opportunity to put a distinctive and personal stamp on the residence. The original staircase consisted of an

This exceptional, hairy-paw-footed eighteenth-century secretary cabinet was made in England to imitate Chinese lacquer, and was presented to the Portuguese royal family. The gilt-bronze escutcheons had to be soaked in water for six months to remove centuries of dirt.

unattractive series of pseudo-Gothic spokes topped by a rickety painted rail. Mr. Netto's longtime friend and decorator, Ann Thornton of Beaumont & Co., suggested enlisting the services of a metallurgist from France, Jean Wiart, who had done restoration work on several important public projects. Wiart was ultimately traced to Paterson, New Jersey, where he operates a foundry.

At the time, M. Wiart was working on the torch for the restoration of the Statue of Liberty and also developing plans for restoring the dome of the Police Building in lower Manhattan. In due course, however, he was persuaded to design a new balustrade for the Netto apartment in Louis XV style. The project proved more challenging than initially anticipated because of the difficult turn in the banister as it ascends to the upper level. When the various components were delivered it was discovered that one of the sections was too long to fit into any of the building's elevators. The piece had to be taken up on foot a total of twenty flights to the penthouse.

Most of the antique furniture and art objects in the duplex came from the Nettos' previous residences. A particularly attractive detail is the use of panels from a rare eighteenth-century lacquer screen from Philippe Farley as double doors leading to both the drawing room and the dining room. In the drawing room, the installed screen doors echo a smaller lacquered screen that once belonged to Mme. Balsan (Consuelo Vanderbilt). A major new acquisition for the drawing room was an eighteenth-century scarlet lacquer secretary cabinet by Gikes Grendy with huge carved and gilded hairy paw feet, found at Glenn Randall. Of special note is a rare antique Aubusson carpet and a Georgian crystal chandelier of magnificent quality and majestic scale. The unusual carved curtain poles and finials in the drawing room—original to the apartment—now support luxurious swags of striped silk made exclusively for Cowtan & Tout by a weaver in Como, Italy. The formal yet comfortable drawing room also acquired a singularly low mantel because a large Venetian glass mirror takes up most of the wall height. Fortunately, the elaborately carved frame of the mirror flows over the crown molding, and the two pieces fit with a quarter of an inch to spare.

Naturally, all the fabrics and wallpapers in the apartment are from Cowtan & Tout. For instance, in the renovated kitchen Netto has used one of the most expensive papers in the world—which, he admits, would only make sense to someone in the business! Napoleonic bee wallpaper lines his bathroom. Even in a closet is a Fortuny-inspired silvery

An opulent staircase linking two floors was designed and made in 1987 by Jean Wiart of Les Metaliers Corporation in Paterson, New Jersey. Surrounding walls have been given a stone block effect.

In the dining room, lacquered Chinese screens are used both as doors and to conceal the exit to the kitchen. An eighteenth-century Venetian glass mirror hangs over a side table. The rug is a thirty-six-foot-long simple striped nineteenth-century kilim that Netto owned and finally cut down to size after keeping it folded over for six months to make sure it worked in the room. Draped silk curtains are of Cowtan & Tout fabric.

Behind a cushion-laden, custom-made sofa covered in Cowtan & Tout Italian silk damask is a rare Régence carved and painted mirror that came from Ruth Constantino's now defunct shop The Connoisseur. Surrounding it are eighteenth-century Italian drawings.

When the Nettos moved in, the fireplace wall in the paneled library was covered in red silk and the fireplace filled with a TV set. The Grinling Gibbonesque boiseries hung over the red silk. Netto assumed there would be paneling underneath but found none. New paneling was made to match the rest of the room. The mantel is from Danny Alesandro. Chintz used for curtains and armchair is Cowtan & Tout's Trees. The carpet is Tabriz, 1875. The French nineteenth-century pastel over the mantel is signed E. Baraize. A door leads to a tiny bar, still lined with the original red silk and mirrors.

A profusion of plants in wooden tubs, terra-cotta pots, and window boxes transforms the terraces of this duplex penthouse into urban gardens. *(above and overleaf)*

gray documentary paper that Netto is interested in reviving. Since both he and his son David are fascinated by architecture and interior design, the library, study, and bedside tables are crammed with books on these subjects. Most of the pictures on the walls are architectural drawings, Old Master drawings, or botanical prints. Of these last, Netto

owns some unusually large ones from seventeenth-century folios—colored at a later date—with printed text on the reverse shadowing through the paper.

The Nettos' passionate interest in the decorative arts has been applied to every detail of their New York penthouse with splendid results.

CLINTON HILL CLASSICISM

Many Manhattanites—and Brook-lynites, too—go through life without a clue as to where Clinton Hill is; yet this was once a remarkably fashionable neighborhood. Though it fell on hard times after 1898 when the five boroughs were merged into Greater New York, many of Clinton Hill's illustrious families remained in their mansions until World War I. After that the maintenance of large residences became difficult, as servants were increasingly hard to find.

The Borough of Brooklyn, or Breuckelen (broken land), as the Dutch named it, started as separate villages that sprang up at important crossroads. Eventually these villages merged. Brooklyn's terrain is mostly flat, so its high points are easily recognizable by their names—Brooklyn Heights, Cobble Hill, Bay Ridge, Park Slope, Prospect Heights, Boerum Hill, Stuyvesant Heights, and Clinton Hill. Named after Governor De Witt Clinton, Clinton Hill overlooks Wallabout Bay and the Brooklyn Navy Yard on the East River. The hill was part of a parcel of land purchased from the Indians by the Dutch in the early 1600s. The parcel was divided into three large farms, granted by patent in the early 1640s by Governor Willem Kieft of Nieuw Amsterdam. During the Revolutionary War, the hill became the site of a British redoubt, influencing Washington's decision to withdraw his troops to Manhattan.

By 1850 most of the hill had been laid out into streets. In the nineteenth century, when yellow fever and cholera were killer diseases, it was believed that the higher up you lived, the more likely you were to remain healthy. Clinton and Washington avenues, at the apex of Clinton Hill, were therefore the most desirable thoroughfares and attracted many of New York's leading families: the Arbuckles (sugar and coffee); Bristols (Bristol-Meyer); Jenningses (lace manufacturing); Liebmans (Rheingold Breweries); Otises (Otis Elevators); Pratts, Bedfords, and Pouches (partners in Standard Oil); Pfizers (drug manufacturers); Reynoldses (aluminum); Sperrys (Sperry-Rand); and Underwoods (Underwood Typewriters). The affluent lived on the wide, tree-lined avenues atop the hill, while adjacent parallel streets were devoted largely to carriage houses, servants' quarters, and more modest brownstones.

The Pratts were the most influential of these families. The first Pratt mansion was erected on Clinton Avenue in 1875, and over the next quarter century four other mansions were built nearby as wedding presents to Pratt offspring. The family name lives on today in New York's notable college of art, architecture, engineering, and library sciences—the Pratt Institute. It was founded in 1887 by Charles Pratt, a partner of John D. Rockefeller in the Standard Oil Company. The eighteen-acre campus, its green spaces, cultural activities, college buildings, and use of otherwise obsolete mansions still sets the artistic tone of the neighborhood.

One Pratt student, John Kelley of Knoxville, Tennessee, came to study architecture. He found lodgings close to the institute and soon became fascinated by the architectural variety of the neighborhood. Federal, Greek Revival, and Gothic Revival houses, Italianate frame villas, classic Victorian brownstones, and Romanesque mansions with cast terra-cotta trimmings are all represented. Students did not have to travel far to study the gamut of American nineteenth-century architectural styles.

Kelley's first and unwavering aesthetic love is for the Classical style. Fifteen years ago, however, when he was a student, this passion was well-nigh subversive. For everyone else, Bauhaus International

Leading off the hall is a small kitchen. A trompe l'oeil painting in the seventeenth-century manner shows three macaws at a window with a draped curtain. The marble bust is of Caesar Augustus—one of the most copied of the Roman busts in the eighteenth and nineteenth centuries. It was bought at auction.

was the Mies *en scene*. Kelley ran athwart his teachers but held to his beliefs. He is somewhat vindicated now that the Post-Modernists (or Neo-neon-Classicists) have joined the parade.

Kelley worked as an architect for several years, bucking the Bauhaus trendies. His mother allowed him to "classicize" the family house in Tennessee, but he was drawn toward the more personally controllable art of painting. Eventually making the decision to paint, he celebrated by buying a bronze statuette of the Winged Victory (a nineteenth-century copy from the Archaeological Museum in Naples) and signed on at the Art Students' League in New York. He has never regretted the decision. Though the bulk of his income comes from portrait painting, he has gradually put together an impressive collection of paintings based on Classical subjects.

Kelley remained in the Clinton Hill neighborhood and has witnessed the gradual upgrading of the area. Every day he sees houses being restored and repaired by those who care about Clinton Hill's architectural heritage. It was recently declared a historic district.

Kelley lives on one of the grand streets, Washington Avenue, in an apartment he once shared as a student. He is fortunate to have as a landlord photographer Erik Falkensteen, who is equally enthusiastic about the architecture of the neighborhood.

Kelley's small, floor-through apartment is in a brownstone row house built in the 1870s. Among its virtues are original—and very fancy compared with today's offerings—parquet floors, shutters, ceiling moldings, and marble fireplaces. The shells of these houses were built on speculation, allowing buyers to pick the floor patterns and fireplaces they preferred from a variety of designs. Kelley knew he would be using the apartment as both a residence and a studio, so he commandeered part of the L-shaped front parlor as his workroom. In the late 1950s or early 1960s, plaster had been removed from one wall, exposing the brick. This provided an agreeable background for a studio, so he merely gave it a coat of white paint. The rest of the room is formally plastered and allows plenty of space for a small dining table, a collection of interesting chairs, and wall space to hang paintings. His paintings, which feature the human form—a rarity in today's living spaces—blend with his Classical furnishings and sleight-of-hand décor. Confronted with mythical scenes of ancient gods and goddesses, one is transported to another world. The idealized

In the bedroom, the bronze wrestler in the foreground, the Winged Victory on the headboard, and the Hermes atop the 1820s walnut cabinet are all nineteenth-century replicas from the Archaeological Museum in Naples. The signed klismos chairs are by American designer T. H. Robsjohn-Gibbings, who designed a line of archaeologically correct Greek-inspired furniture. The seats are of leather thongs.

In the bathroom the shower is concealed behind a painted screen. The female nude was painted by Kelley while at the Art Students' League. (He had arrived late to class and this was the only view of the model left.) The overscaled frame was found on the sidewalk. The 1830s American burl maple chair, given as a housewarming present, once allegedly belonged to Katharine Hepburn. Reflected in the mirror is a study of a man dating from Kelley's Art Students' League days.

nudes, flowing draperies, and heightened colors are in the direct tradition of David and Ingres, of Watts, Leighton, and Alma-Tadema, and of the twentieth-century work of Rex Whistler. These are Kelley's idols, and he is unabashed in his acknowledgment of their influence. To create a "Classical" interior in a tiny space is a challenge requiring panache and drama. He has amassed European and American furniture, but all in compatible styles, be it a French Empire chair or an American twentieth-century klismos chair by T. H. Robsjohn-Gibbings (author of Goodbye Mr. Chippendale, a scathing book on fashionable decorators of the 1940s). He has added faux touches where necessary—granite-painted bases, marble tabletops, a painted floor cloth, a trompe l'oeil window.

To disguise a meager hallway, striped cotton (a bargain from 14th Street in Manhattan) was simply flung—unhemmed, leaving the selvage as edging—over dowel rods. Part of it is looped back, held by a precious piece of antique gold lace, to serve as the entrance to the kitchen. On the opposite side, the curtains conceal a coat closet. To help dramatize the tiny hall, Kelley painted a canvas floor cloth with marble tiles, in the American nineteenth-century tradition, and gave it several coats of polyurethane. The ceiling light fixture is a nineteenth-century bronze lamp with a celestial globe bought at an auction and wired by Kelley.

Furniture has been invented. In his bedroom, which has a pleasant view of his landlord's garden, a desk has been concocted from a marbleized hollow door set on two filing cabinets. Homemade bookshelves have been marbleized black and edged with antiqued gold braid gleaned in New York's garment district. Kelley designed a monolithic bed flanked by shelves, which was made by his brother, who owns a woodworking shop.

The apartment is punctuated with objects from the late eighteenth and early nineteenth centuries, all in the New Classical style. In its day, this style influenced all of Europe as well as America. Fashionable houses displayed reproductions of braziers for burning incense, vessels for oil, votive heads, ceremonial drinking cups, pyramids, romantically ruined marble columns, and bronze figurines. These replicas of ancient Greek and Roman artifacts were made in response to the rediscoveries of the ancient world. Many of them were correct copies from pieces in the Naples Museum, which held the copyright for reproduction during most of the nineteenth century—rather like (if one can bear the comparison) today's Franklin Mint. Kelley avidly collects these objects and, indeed, anything related to them. Even in his kitchen one discovers cans of olive oil chosen for their Classical connotations—one labeled Hermes and another, Diana. In his quiet, soft-spoken way, John Kelley is as determined as ever to pursue his particular direction.

Tea is served in cups copied from an eighteenth-century Italian pattern called Ercolano, by Richard Ginori. The Spode sugar bowl and cream jug were made in these classical forms until the end of the nineteenth century. The screen depicts the Metropolitan Museum as a Classical ruin.

Kelley's studio is dominated by his painting *Oedipus and the Sphinx*. To the right is his *Persephone*, her mythical pomegranate echoed by two dried pomegranates on the table below. Made from a painted wood slab, the table is set on two monopodium gold-leafed lions with faux granite bases. On the wall to the left is a self-portrait.

In the dining area two Charles X chairs are covered in striped Indian silk found on Orchard Street. A French Empire armchair is upholstered in a red, apparently indestructible, preplastic leatherette, circa 1910. The original marble mantel holds early-nineteenth-century neoclassical objects. The original parquet floor is partly covered with a wool Dhurrie rug. Kelley's paintings—*Hercules with Queen Omphale* and *Bacchus*—on one side of the room are balanced on the other by a painted screen concealing his canvases. Sphinx heads decorate the velvet-covered early-nineteenth-century sofa. Against the wall are early-nineteenth-century French chairs with added ormolu ornamentation.

CHIC CHINOISERIE

Mr. and Mrs. Thomas L. Kempner have lived in the same duplex for some thirty-three years, a long time for those on Manhattan's social merry-go-round. On the Upper East Side, their apartment is in a building constructed in the late twenties and early thirties — the heyday of large and luxurious apartment houses.

When Nan Kempner first arrived in New York from San Francisco, she turned to decorator Billy Baldwin, by then at the top of his profession, to help organize her first apartment. His touch remains, in pieces of furniture that have been incorporated throughout the duplex. Among the souvenirs of his work are his signature brass-poled bookshelves, which now grace a mirrored workout room, though Mrs. Kempner is not quite sure whether the urbane designer would have wholly approved. No one decorator — and there have been several over the years — has totally influenced Nan Kempner. Indeed, she feels it might be the other way around — yet no designer she has worked with has failed to leave a lasting mark on her own style.

For the first few years of their married life, the Kempners lived in England. It was there that Nan started collecting porcelain birds, always in pairs, an agglomeration that continues to grow — despite her murmurs that she can no longer afford them. The most recently added are *blanc de Chine* cockerels that now adorn the Kempners' dining room table. The Antique Porcelain Company in London was her alma mater in this realm.

When Nan was pregnant with her third child, the Kempners moved to the duplex. On a vacation in Palm Springs, she ran into a San Francisco chum, interior designer Michael Taylor, who had developed a new and excitingly casual style of décor. Inspired by thirties decorator Syrie Maugham (wife of Somerset Maugham), he translated her passion for the all-white room into a particularly Californian look, bringing in lush plants and greenery to soften the dazzling West Coast light. His use of overscaled wicker, quarry-tile flooring, natural colors, stripped-and-bleached log, cast stone, rattan or sandstone furniture, adobe construction mingled with simple bunkhouse architecture, combined with an echo of the forties, was innovative, stimulating, and very West Coast.

Mrs. Kempner told Michael Taylor about the new duplex and together they went over the floor plan. Very quickly they agreed on a wish list. Returning to New York they set about methodically finding the hoped-for furnishings. Amazingly, in two days they fell upon exactly the right carpets, mirrors, chests, and other furniture that was in keeping with the scale of the duplex and the look they desired.

Michael Taylor's typical San Francisco style had to be modified for the Manhattan apartment, where an open, indoor-outdoor way of living is impossible. The only room that bears his California stamp is the television room, which used to be the nursery. Typical Taylor touches are the low, polished quarry-stone tables and the large-scale rattan furniture juxtaposed against red, black, and white seventeenth-century Japanese paper screens. The room also contains a silk-screen portrait of Nan Kempner by Andy Warhol.

It was obvious that the Kempners' sizable drawing room lent itself to large groups. Taylor's plan included upholstered banquettes — something that caused raised eyebrows among Manhattanites three decades ago, though they not only provide functional, relaxed seating but also have taken on

In the Kempners' elevator lobby a plinth holding a stylized head by Emilio Greco, 1956, is flanked by scallop shell sconces and faux leopard-seated, faux bamboo chairs.

an almost period charm. Typical of Michael Taylor's forties-inspired decoration are leopard-skin cushions and small armchairs with legs resembling huge tasseled ropes. In his original scheme these chairs were upholstered in black, but they have since been re-covered by Mark Hampton in rich brown velvet.

The acquisition of some outstanding painted Chinese silk panels established the main theme of the duplex. These panels, which were bought from the estate of a friend of Mrs. Kempner's grand-mother, enhance the Kempners' dining room—considered one of the prettiest in New York. Por-celain birds, arranged above the fireplace, augment the Chinese panels, which depict birds and butter-flies flitting in and out of grafted trees tied with ribbons. An unusually lavish matching dinner set of Chinese Export porcelain fits in perfectly, and is displayed in a glass-fronted cabinet opposite the fireplace. A faux wood-grained paint finish blends these elements together. The room is anchored by a rare French needlepoint carpet portraying mythical griffins in brilliant colors. Lacquered Chinese screens hide the doorway to the pantry and kitchen. The dining room is used not only at night, when the chandelier's real candles are lit, but also in the morning; Mr. Kempner begins his day here with

juice and the *Wall Street Journal* before heading off to Loeb Partners.

The chinoiserie motif was extended when Nan Kempner came across a huge twelve-panel coro-mandel screen that fit easily along the length of the drawing room. For some twenty years she searched for the perfect overmantel. Finally, antiquarian Nor-ton Rosenbaum found what she had been looking for: a carved and gilded Chinese Chippendale mir-rored overmantel—complete with appropriate Man-darin figure and ho-ho birds—together with what is possibly its original ormolu-embellished marble mantel. Chinese bibelots, including carved green quartz and pale green jade ornaments, and pieces of turquoise blue Ming dot the side tables in the drawing room, *objets* that Mrs. Kempner arranges to the millimeter. Housekeeping here is a zealous business. Every week the rooms are thoroughly swept and garnished as if it were the annual spring cleaning. Serious, too, is the art. Works by such painters as Picasso, Matisse, and Signac fill the wall space that is not taken up by the coromandel screen, mirrors, carved wall chandeliers, or windows.

The entrance hall gets its share of the Chinese touch in the form of a huge lacquered chest. A *bureau plat* stands on a Russian runner that once

The bird-and-tree theme of the din-ing room was established by the seventeenth-century Chinese silk panels. This theme is repeated in Mrs. Kempner's collection of pairs of porcelain birds, including the *blanc de Chine* cockerels on the table. The woodwork surrounding the silk panels is finished in faux graining. On the floor is a vibrant French needlepoint carpet depicting griffins. On either side of the fireplace are ceramic torchères resembling outsize shells and coral.

belonged to Nan Kempner's mother. Also from her San Francisco house are two French seventeenth-century carved-wood cartouches. One depicts an assemblage of artifacts used in the theater and the other, farming implements.

Off the hall is the library, a warm, cozy den with glazed walls, comfortable chintz-covered sofas, plenty of books, and interesting paintings, including an unusual Magritte over the fireplace, *Paysage en feu*, which thrilled the author of Magritte's catalogue raisonné. On the desk and side tables are thoughtful mixtures of such disparate objects as Battersea boxes, Chinese animals, treen (polished wood) apples and pears, and a Dutch eighteenth-century chinoiserie leather screen. The windows are covered with a bamboo shade.

The guest wing, on the same floor as the entrance hall, gives the visitor privacy. "No one wants to leave," admits Mrs. Kempner. The guest bedroom is lined in hand-painted Chinese wallpaper and has two four-posters covered with apricot linen into which green and white dots are woven. The pretty adjoining bathroom is furnished with a bamboo-and-glass makeup table invented by Michael Taylor, a draped tub, and Chinese bibelots.

A powder room, enveloped in heavy, Roman-striped cotton faille, is fitted with gold hardware in the shape of hands. Drawing back the curtain that conceals the toilet, one unexpectedly comes upon a number of Matisse drawings on the walls.

A staircase curves up to the bedroom floor. The corridor leading to the master bedroom displays a set of Dutch seventeenth-century colored botanical drawings and a series of drawings by Pissarro. Another antique hand-painted Chinese wallpaper, this one with a green ground, lines the master bedroom. Mrs. Kempner is known for her simple, tailored clothes; in the bedroom, however, she can indulge another side of her personality—feminine lace and embroidered bed linen. Near the bed are piles of books, easy-to-reach telephones, pencils, and notepaper, for this is where Mrs. Kempner starts her day with breakfast on a tray and the bed as an office. A diminutive velour-covered sofa is laden with silken pillows. More stacks of books sit on a table in front of the fireplace, which is often lit. A pair of Irish mirrors face each other across the room. They are hung above eighteenth-century painted Venetian chests of drawers, on which are groups of silver-framed photographs of family and

On one side of the drawing room is a twelve-panel coromandel screen. Corduroy-covered buttoned banquettes, outrageously modern when first designed by Michael Taylor thirty-three years ago, are perfect for seating groups of guests. The Chinese Chippendale mirror and mantel had been on Mrs. Kempner's wish list for twenty years before they were unearthed in London.

A powder room off the entrance hall is draped entirely in Roman-striped cotton faille. Cocteauesque brass faucets of hands embellish the marble washstand. The becurtained toilet beyond is hung with framed Matisse drawings.

Glazed Ming-red walls, dark floral chintz, and a Dutch eighteenth-century chinoiserie leather screen help give the library a cozy feeling.

One of the most recently organized rooms in the duplex is the dressing room, designed by Chessy Rayner of Mac II. In lieu of closets it is draped in printed cotton. Huge fans conceal the lights. Though Nan Kempner's wardrobe is predominantly neutral-colored, on the settee is a gold lamé jacket from Yves Saint Laurent.

friends. Chinese figures of the immortals decorate the mantel.

Since Michael Taylor's death, another decorator has worked on revamping Mrs. Kempner's dressing room. Chessy Rayner of Mac II concocted a curtained boudoir, every woman's dream place. With room enough to accommodate a masseur's table, a sofa to lay out clothes, an armchair, and a side table, the effect is feminine without being in the least frilly. Nan Kempner's wardrobe of mostly black and beige tailored clothes from her favorite couturiers is hidden behind yards of effective but not madly expensive printed-cotton curtains. Large fans diffuse and conceal the lights, and antique mirrors add refinement.

Mrs. Kemper's dressing room and a workout

room took over what were originally children's rooms. The gym is mirrored and filled with exercise machines that both Mr. and Mrs. Kempner use, obviously to great effect! Model-slender, groomed, and maintained as efficiently as the apartment, Mrs. Kempner works for Christie's, where she is able to steer her wide range of friends toward the many delights of that auction house. She says the job in turn provides her with a wonderful learning experience.

The apartment was given "good bones," as Nan Kempner says, by Michael Taylor. "It hasn't really changed except for the nursery and children's rooms being made over into rooms that Tommy and I use—the TV room, the dressing room, and the gym. Otherwise it's just been added to and, I hope, improved over the years. It's a happy house."

HARLEM
FANTASY

Harlem is famous the world over as the capital of American black culture. This wasn't always so. Named Nieuw Haarlem after the Dutch town of Haarlem, the region was farmland until well into the nineteenth century. When Manhattan's grid plan was first proposed in 1807, New Yorkers found the idea of the city spreading up to 155th Street laughable. In 1879, however, when elevated rapid transit extended up the West Side, real estate speculators thought the area above 110th Street, known as Morningside Heights and Hamilton Heights, would become *the* place for well-to-do families to settle.

Morningside Heights is dominated by the presence of Columbia University, Barnard College, and the Cathedral of St. John the Divine, all of which were begun before the turn of the century. Just to the north is Hamilton Heights, later also called Sugar Hill, which includes City College and the old village of Manhattanville. Before being built up, the region was scattered with prosperous country estates, including that of Alexander Hamilton, after whom the area is named. His house, Hamilton Grange, an 1802 Federal wood-frame structure, is a miraculous survivor, now wedged sideways between St. Luke's Episcopal Church and an apartment building. Since 1974, the area centered around Convent Avenue between 141st and 145th streets has been designated a historic district.

From 1880 onward picturesque row houses sprang up on the new streets to attract downtown gentry. These were designed and decorated in a variety of pseudo-period styles, including Flemish, Tudor, and Romanesque. This speculative building rush was slowed by a small crash in the 1890s, and halted completely by the financial panic of

1904. Subsequent buildings never equalled the area's original grandeur despite the opening of the subway on the West Side in 1906. Substantial houses intended for upper-class life gradually became inhabited by middle-class families, mostly of German and Irish descent.

The financial crunch caused many houses to be broken up into boardinghouses. As black families were priced out of the west side of midtown by commercial development they moved north to Harlem, where they were welcomed by landlords with vacant apartments. The better off came to Sugar Hill and Striver's Row, giving these places vibrant and definitive characters. By the twenties, Harlem had become a magnet for ambitious, original, and talented blacks.

Within the historic district of Hamilton Heights is a row of four town houses built between 1894 and 1896 for Charles J. Judson. They were designed by architect Clarence F. True, who made a name for himself designing some highly personal versions of neo-Elizabethan Renaissance houses along Riverside Drive. The four Harlem row houses have his signature mix of stylistic motifs: bas-relief panels, swags, putti decorating the string course above the limestone first story, and bowed-front upper stories of buff-colored brick. While hinting at the Italianate style, the balustrades and window surrounds impart decorative François I overtones.

Interior designers Timothy Van Dam and Ronald Wagner bought one of these houses a few years ago. Previously a boardinghouse, the place had been allowed to fall into a sad condition. Restoring the house while carrying on their full-time design practices and teaching has been no mean feat. But the dwelling has come alive again and, what's more, taken on a romantic charm that it probably never had before.

The original tiles in this bathroom are bordered with a shell motif. The plant stand and chair are Gothic Revival. Reflected in the medicine cabinet mirror is a sketch of a man done at the Philadelphia Academy of Art in 1909.

The first owner was Dr. Ernest J. Lederle, a New York health commissioner and founder of Lederle Laboratories, which today is a division of the American Cyanamid Co. He bought the newly built house in 1896 for $15,000. The Lederles had one daughter, Mary, and her room near the top of the house can be identified by its fire grate, which is decorated with the figure of a little girl. The room now serves as Van Dam's design office; Wagner runs his design business from an office downtown.

Originally the house was lit with gas chandeliers and wall sconces, and heated by a forced-air system with additional heat from gaslit fires. Six of the seven fireplaces retain their original decorative bronze interiors, marble surrounds, and ceramic logs, which are fitted with gas jets, so that at the touch of a match one can cozy up to a convincing "period" fire. Mantels feature elaborate architectural detailing supported by columns, indicating that the house was exceptionally sumptuous when built. Central heating and electricity were put in later, but when the present owners moved in they discovered that the whole house had electricity sufficient only for an average studio apartment. All five floors and basement were rewired.

From the low-ceilinged foyer a flight of stairs ascends to a grand, high-ceilinged hall screened by a triple-arched Ionic arcade. As the hall floor was in a state of collapse, the owners replaced it with marble. A dramatic, cloud-painted oculus in the ceiling is backlit by a tiny strip of light hidden behind a plaster molding. By great good luck, they rescued an eleven-and-a-half-foot mirror of mercury-silvered glass, circa 1880, as it was about to be broken up and carted off.

A newly restored sliding door leads to the drawing room, with its pair of tall windows overlooking the street. Here curtains of unhemmed, unbleached muslin are draped with panache. A Herez carpet dresses the oak-and-mahogany parquet floor. A mirrored overmantel is flanked by columns that are echoed on the onyx-surrounded fireplace

The hall floor is of white marble inset with verd antique squares. The table holds a collection of marble and glass balls and an alabaster dish. Gilt-bronze-decorated 1865 hall chairs of ebonized cherry with rosewood and gilt inlay are by the New York firm Pottier & Stymus. The seats retain their original velvet. Sliding doors lead to both the drawing room and dining room.

The dining room chandelier came from Sister Pugh's thrift shop, the hurricane shades from Buffalo. On the mantel an 1880s Egyptian Revival clock is flanked by drinking horns in the shape of winged animals from Brighton, England; late-Victorian candlesticks; and anthemion roof details from Athens. The corner cemetery urn had to be stripped of radiator paint.

The drawing room mantel holds a Victorian marble Diana, Meissen and Parian ware statuettes and busts, French Empire candlesticks, and white marble urns. The American glass-eyed wood cherub above was probably meant to be gilded. A round picture of the seasons hangs over a "minute" painting in the corner, above a painted crackle-finished commode. A bronze Hermes and a discus thrower stand on the table in the foreground.

Until the right bed comes along, a mattress is made up on the floor of this otherwise quite grand bedroom. On the right a Federal mirror hangs over a painted card table. The 1870 hooked carpet runner is American. The American Empire chest (with a bonnet drawer!) was made in New York City, circa 1830. Its marble top, found separately, fit exactly.

below. In a labor of love, Van Dam applied and burnished twenty-two-karat gold leaf to the picture rail above. In one corner, a "minute" painting hangs in its gilt frame. In the nineteenth century, such paintings were dashed off in a minute just to sell the elaborate frames. A gilded spool chair nestles in the curve of the piano. An armchair, rescued from a Dumpster, has Russian/Regency roots and has been repaired and reupholstered in figured satin. It is at home in this room, though most of the furniture here and throughout the house is American Empire.

The dining room leads off the other side of the hall. It, too, can be closed off by a large sliding door, which gives Van Dam and Wagner a chance to create dramatic effects when they entertain — which is quite often and to much acclaim. They are

keen cooks, so the first thing they moved into the kitchen beyond the dining room was a Garland stove. The dining room has chest-high wainscoting and an imposing mantel of quarter-sawn oak.

A legacy from the former landlady, throughout much of the house, and especially on the bedroom floor, is an eccentric wall treatment. Though well into her eighties, she painstakingly finger-painted the walls with joint compound, then added swirls of paint. As this "fantasy finish" is far from their taste, Van Dam and Wagner will deal with it eventually, but in the meantime they are learning to live with it. As yet, the ideal bed for the master bedroom has not been found, so the temporary solution, as for many New Yorkers, is simply a mattress on the floor.

The bathroom remains very much as it was

when built. The original shell pattern borders the lower, tiled part of the room. A nonelectric ceiling lamp is romantically lit with a candle for parties.

Another large bedroom on this floor has been converted into the library and will eventually be lined in antique paneling. For now, standard industrial metal bookshelves are in use. The ornate curtains, swankily lined in silk, were purchased at Everybody's Thrift Shop on Park Avenue South. The room contains enough travel souvenirs, mementos, and bric-a-brac to suit turn-of-the-century taste: There is a Tibetan monk's box intended for prayer scrolls, a Tibetan pilgrim's silver lamp that burns yak butter, a bundle of incense from the Potala monastery, a scrimshaw walrus tusk, a worn leopard skin, a beat-up ebonized Eastlake chair with a fancy dress crown tossed jauntily over one side. Behind a sofa is an architectural model of the police department headquarters on Lafayette Street made by Van Dam when a student at Pratt. Apart from the grand curtains, the room is dominated by two white columns with elaborate capitals that flank the already fancy fireplace. The columns were rescued from the garbage by Wagner's father in Buffalo and the capitals were found at auction.

On the floor above are more bedrooms and another bathroom that would once have been used by servants. Over these rooms is an attic floor.

The back of the house overlooks a garden, formerly used as a drying yard. The owners have laid terraces and planted flowers and shrubs. A fountain punctuates the scheme, and in the summer a cupid that was found in the house is positioned outside as the genius of the place.

Both owners enjoy all the hard work that has gone into the rehabilitation of the Harlem habitat. As enthusiastic members of the Hamilton Heights Homeowners Association, they are interested in both the history and vigor of the neighborhood and open their house to visitors on fund-raising tours. As designers, they have pulled together a very large house with flair, fantasy, and improvisation, a good example of what *Vogue* used to describe as "More Taste Than Money." They comb thrift and antique shops, especially those in Harlem, such as Sister Pugh's or Akbar, and in Wagner's hometown of Buffalo, New York, which they claim is a treasure trove of turn-of-the-century artifacts. They rescue furniture that less imaginative folk throw out, and rehabilitate it, to the envy of their friends and neighbors.

On the mantel in the library are a figure of Socrates, Tibetan prayer beads, Victorian trophies, and above, a terra-cotta gargoyle. A Federal pier glass hangs between the windows. On the foreground table is a piano scarf of voided velvet and a marble figure of the Dying Gaul. The columns came from Buffalo and the capitals from an auction upstate.

SOHO LOFT

Until the 1960s, most SoHo lofts were occupied by small manufacturing businesses, and few were lawful residences. Nowadays they are not only valid living spaces but some rate highly on New York's ever-changing and competitive scale of style and taste.

One SoHo loft, though designed in 1980, remains highly desirable to this day. It comprises the top floor of a century-old building that had been used in the past for making a variety of products, including navigational equipment (during World War II) and shoes, and later, as a showroom for flowers and plants. When owner Hans Peter Weiss bought the space, there was still a brick floor in one part of the loft—a feature that Weiss incorporated into his overall design.

Weiss, creative art director with a Swiss-based international advertising agency, was working in New York when he bought and renovated the loft. He himself designed the apartment, using an architect only for help on technical and structural details. A problem common to most lofts in New York is that of bringing water into and out of more than one place per floor. Weiss, whose plan included two separate bathrooms on opposite sides of the loft, as well as a central kitchen, eventually solved this problem by enclosing waste pipes in an inner core and raising the floor of the master bedroom.

The unassuming entrance to the building belies the sophisticated closed-circuit television system that monitors all visitors. In the loft's lobby, which is covered with gray industrial carpeting, is a large walk-in coat closet, a floor-to-ceiling wine rack, and a battery of electronic devices—including the screen showing passersby on the street—and light switches with dimmers to set the mood.

The main room of the loft—part studio, part living room—gives the impression of a great white space lit on three sides by deeply recessed, arched windows and from above by three large skylights. Reflected light bounces off white walls, ceiling, and the shiny white painted wood floor. White ceiling fans circulate the air. Structural columns, common to many lofts built in the late nineteenth century, have been marbleized in a warm, creamy beige, a finish that is repeated on one very large and several smaller simple coffee tables. Comfortable sofas and armchairs are upholstered and cushioned in heavy white-on-white striped cotton, and this fabric covers even the rounded casters on which they stand. Track lighting on the ceiling provides additional directional light, and between each window a translucent quarter-sphere throws diffused light upward. Standing by a column near the entrance is an intriguing sculpture of a clown and a pig. It is based on a German folk tale and made by Erich Bödeker, a German artist who worked in the Ruhr mines. Some of the windowsills contain boxes of ivy that has crept along the arches, forming almost complete circles of greenery. On the south side of the room are movable potted palms and great, bark-encrusted containers of Boston ferns hanging from the ceiling. These have been in place since the completion of the renovation and are kept green by constant care and mist from a humidifier. A delicate white Tim Prentice mobile hangs from one of the skylights—a present from photographer Neal Slavin. In one corner, a raised, gray-carpeted platform becomes a modern version of a Turkish corner. Above it hangs a white-cushioned hammock, a perfect place to read, laze, or just gaze out the window at the changing face of the neighborhood.

In the opposite corner, partly screened by the

Two of the arched windows in the studio are almost completely circled in ivy. Structural pillars are marbleized. The sculpture of a clown and a pig depicts a German folk tale and is by Erich Bödeker, who used to work in the Ruhr mines.

The living room is lit on three sides by arched windows, and by overhead skylights. Hanging from one skylight is a mobile by Tim Prentice. Sofas upholstered in white-on-white striped cotton surround a coffee table that is marbleized to match the columns.

In contrast to the lightness of the rest of this loft, the walls and floor of the master bathroom are covered with dark gray tiles. Stainless steel fittings, and navy, white, and gray towels complement the room.

wall enclosing the stairwell and coat closet, is the media space. Wall shelves contain books—many on art and many in German—records, tapes, television, and stereo system. Jutting out from the wall is a sizable writing desk made by Weiss's cousin, Yvo Buchli. Its knee space forms an arch that echoes the arched windows of the room. This semicircular arched motif recurs throughout the loft, notably in a pair of doors also made by Buchli that lead to a couple of bedrooms on the north side of the floor. A fireplace, frequently used in the winter, is surrounded by contemporary paintings and prints.

To the left of the entrance is the kitchen area. It is surrounded by a counter covered with white Formica tiles that also cover a conveniently placed bench with cubbyholes below where one can temporarily dump packages or sit to change shoes.

Everything in the white-tiled kitchen is built in, including two refrigerators, a counter dishwasher, a disposal unit set into the counter, a car radio, sound-system controls, and drawers so ingeniously concealed they are well-nigh invisible! A Garland stove with heavy iron pots and two sinks with high taps useful for filling oversized vases are other features. Semisphere-shaped shades resembling great hair dryers throw light onto the counters. The original sprinkler pipes and structural pillars have been retained, adding a loftlike character to the space.

Close to the kitchen area is a long oval, polished-granite dining table made by Forno Marble in Long Island. Between the windows in this part of the studio, niches hold collected pieces of sculpture and pottery.

Next to a wall hung with six Andy Warhol

In the kitchen white Formica tiles cover the counters and the bench. On the wall leading to the workroom is a series of Andy Warhol Marilyns.

Marilyns is a passage leading to the guest bedroom area. On the left of the passage is a photographic darkroom. On the right are closets containing household utilities, including industrial cleaning equipment. The passage widens into a room almost filled by a professional cutting table, complete with drawers for findings and space below to stack fabric. Previously used by a fashion designer friend, it is now useful as a table for selecting, cutting, and matting photographs. On the walls are black-and-white photographs of SoHo characters—street musicians, maids, actors, tourists—taken by Carolyn Jones, who uses the loft as a studio once in a while. On one side of the room is a full, white-tiled bathroom, with gray towels and stainless steel accents. A white-painted, custom-made metal staircase leads up from this room to the roof garden.

A major part of Weiss's renovation took place on the roof. The floor was carefully planned and executed, using as a motif a series of huge wooden triangles, each of which can be lifted up to service the area underneath. A fantastic, neoclassical greenhouse made of metal-framed transparent triangles sits on the roof and can be used winter or summer as a romantic spot to serve drinks and look out over Manhattan toward the elegant spires of the Empire State and Chrysler buildings to the north. To the south is a view of Wall Street and the twin towers

of the World Trade Center. When the greenhouse is used as a *jardin d'hiver*, heat comes up through the stairwell. When not in use, a transparent plastic trap door blocks the heat.

Beyond the cutting room are a pair of bedrooms, each one entered through Yvo Buchli's arched, divided doors. They are brick walled and minimally furnished. The floors throughout this area are brick—the shoe factory's legacy—but painted shiny black. Weiss liked the effect, and, to tie it in with his reorganization of the space, he even extended the brick floors.

Another completely separate suite is found on the opposite side of the loft and can be reached only by going through the studio. This wing consists of the master bedroom, an office, a large dark gray-tiled bathroom with a red-lined whirlpool bath that can be completely covered with a tiled lid, and a dark-mirrored dressing room—temporarily, and successfully, converted into a working office, with stationery now sitting in the smart black painted shelves that were once designed to hold shirts.

The apartment is a good example of the advantages of New York loft living. Though it means a downtown address (unthinkable to some New Yorkers), you do get a luxurious amount of space, plus light on all four sides—all in all, not a bad exchange.

In this workroom, with its metal cutting table and shiny black-painted brick floor, black-and-white photographs of neighborhood personalities are by Carolyn Jones. The arched double doors at the far end were made by Weiss's cousin, Yvo Buchli, and lead into two separate bedrooms.

White-painted, custom-made metal stairs lead up to the terrace on the roof. The photograph by Carolyn Jones is of SoHo street cleaner George.

From the dining area, with its black granite custom-made table, can be seen the diagonal stretch of the studio. A frequently used fireplace is on the right wall.

WEST SIDE ARTISTRY

The black-lacquered-and-steel round dining table and bentwood chairs provide a foil for David Hockney's 1978 *Noon Pool with Cloud Reflections*. Nineteenth-century bronze male and female figures hold pineapples, symbols of hospitality. The curved glass wall sculpture, *Stocking Stairs*, 1976, is by Christopher Wilmarth, who had a retrospective at the Museum of Modern Art in 1989.

Though East Siders might not agree, Central Park West, according to the *AIA Guide to New York City*, has "generally maintained an unflagging fashionable quality" from Columbus Circle at 59th Street, where the avenue starts, to 96th Street. The grand West Side apartment buildings are usually far more imaginative than those on the east side of Central Park. One that stands out especially is a French Empire-style building designed by Townsend, Steinle & Haskell and built in 1908. It falls within the Central Park West–76th Street Historic District, and is described in the *AIA Guide* as a "cubical russet brick wedding cake topped by a grand convex mansard roof. The pastry chef's whipped-cream efforts are executed in limestone in the interests of posterity." Columns, of a style never seen on any historic baroque structure, frame the entrance. Pediments and keystones over windows, and swags beneath, are far from classic in proportion but exuberant nonetheless. There are balconies with iron railings on some floors, including the one where Ashton Hawkins—Executive Vice President of the Metropolitan Museum of Art—lives.

When first built, this eclectic building had three apartments per floor. By the time Hawkins moved in, his space was not the full-sized, eight-room apartment of the building's original plan; two rooms—a large living room and dining room—had been taken over by an adjoining apartment. Along with architect Yann Weymouth (who gained his experience in the offices of I. M. Pei, for whom he oversaw the Louvre pyramid project in Paris), Hawkins ingeniously redesigned the space to make it more flexible and appear larger. An air vent ran through the core of the apartment. By painting the interior of the shaft white, and installing translucent window panels, reflected light (artificial at night) was brought into the entrance hall, a coat closet, and a good-sized bathroom.

Two major rooms, described as "chambers" on the original plans, were united into one large living room with a dining area near the kitchen. The wall originally dividing them was removed, leaving a single structural pillar. It has been disguised as an elegant, sponge-painted Doric column. A second, similar column was added for symmetry.

The apartment affords Hawkins ample space to display and enjoy art collected ever since he was a youth. His walls, bookshelves, and side tables are covered with paintings, drawings, photographs, and objects. His collection is varied, but his discernment is constant. One recently acquired painting in the entrance hall is a mid-seventeenth-century Venetian baroque depiction of King David holding a viola da gamba. This painting by an unknown artist might more readily be found lining the hallway of a Venetian palazzo than a New York apartment. In complete contrast—but typical of Hawkins's eclectic bravura—is an ingenuous red-and-black painting of a rowboat by contemporary artist Tom Slaughter. Both of these works—the antique and the contemporary—provide a foil for Steve Hannock's black-lit painting of *The Lightning Field*, a mile-long, kilometer-wide, conceptual art work created in the late 1970s in Quemado, New Mexico, by Walter de Maria under the auspices of the Dia Art Foundation, an organization for which Hawkins is now chairman of the board. Black-and-white photographs by Bruce Weber, Edward Steiglitz, and André Kertész enhance the hall's central pillar. On the walls, drawings by Elizabeth Frink and Helen Frankenthaler and a lithograph by Georgia O'Keeffe combine with an Andy Warhol *Campbell's Soup* T-shirt and a splendid

Navajo second phase chief's blanket.

The entrance hall leads to a corridor lined on both sides with pictures by such artists and photographers as Herbert Ross, Robert Mapplethorpe, Edward Ruscha, Guy Pène duBois, Janet Fish, Bill Brandt, David Hockney, Helen Frankenthaler, Irving Penn, Richard Avedon, Craig McPherson, and Alan Shields. There is also a fragile painted clay vessel with three heads by Brazilian folk artist Odysseus perched on a sophisticated column. Somehow these varied works interact like diverse guests at a good party. The runner carpet was found in central Greece in pristine condition because, though made early in this century as part of a bridal dowry, it was never used.

In the living room a six-panel collage by Bob Smith depicts a camel train making a voyage to the Temple of Dendur—an inside joke, as the temple is now in the Metropolitan Museum. Above it are three fan-shaped sculptures of painted wood by Christopher Hewat. The central one is painted with flowers in turn-of-the-century boudoir style, while those flanking it are more gilded-baroque in feeling. Under a catty-corner window is a Japanese puppet theater probably used by a traveling troupe, bought at the Andy Warhol sale. It is now a receptacle for an assortment of *objets d'art*. On top of it is a Cambodian figure and, hanging above that, a Russian drinking horn.

The living room décor, achieved with the help of Mark Hampton, is done mostly in variations of textured but unobtrusive beige. Tufted-back slipper

In the entrance hall a Venetian baroque painting depicting King David receiving inspiration contrasts with the red boat and pier by Tom Slaughter. In the corridor leading to the living room can be seen Craig McPherson's *Yankee Stadium at Night*, bottom right; Allen Blagdun's *Hill House*, top right; a George Platt Lynes photograph of a male torso, top left; and a Helen Frankenthaler watercolor, bottom left.

chairs are upholstered in *ton sur ton* linen check; a sofa and outsize ottoman are covered in a hexagonal woven fabric; the carpet is composed of pale pastels. All this subdued color serves to show off Hawkins's collection. In one corner, a Regency étagère holds a George Kelly bronze of Icarus falling to earth. Another black light illuminates a Hawkins-commissioned imaginary landscape by Stephen Hannock. Library steps hold more *objets*, as do two Cartier vitrines rescued from the Robert Lehman house and now filled with art and mementos, many of them of Russian origin—Hawkins's mother is Russian.

In the dining area, Hockney's large, six-panel *Noon Pool with Cloud Reflections* virtually propels the eye out the west wall and into the Hudson. The dining table is a circle of black lacquer surrounded by black-lacquered bentwood chairs. Shielding the entrance to the kitchen is a chic, Hampton-designed zebra screen. Between books on the shelves, niches—like wayside shrines—display small pieces of sculpture and pictures. On a table is a photograph of Hawkins's Russian grandmother at a 1912 costume party in St. Petersburg. With more than enough to fill the place, Ashton Hawkins constantly replaces, moves, or replenishes the art works.

The kitchen occupies the same space as it did in the original layout, but appliances, counters, and cupboards have all been updated. Gray granite is used for counters and tabletop; the service entrance door has been stripped down to bare steel, and a built-in steel-fronted refrigerator stands close by, creating a feeling of harmony. A small maid's room beyond the kitchen can accommodate an overnight guest but is generally used as a storage room. When Hawkins moved in, all the woodwork in the apartment was painted. In the process of stripping it down he discovered oak in the kitchen area and mahogany in the larger rooms. Extra mahogany doors taken down during the renovations were converted into swing doors leading to the kitchen from both hall and dining area, and given etched glass windows with round peepholes.

Double doors lead to the master bedroom,

A corridor leading to the living room displays photographs by Avedon, Penn, and Mapplethorpe; two paintings by Ed Ruscha, *Hollywood* and *Double Standard*; and a drawing by David Hockney. In the foreground is a plummeting bronze figure of Icarus by George Kelly.

In the living room, painted wood fan-shaped pieces are by Christopher Hewat. Below them is Bob Smith's *Camel Train*, a procession leading to the Temple of Dendur spread over a series of mixed media panels; some of the camels are cut from Camel cigarette packs.

One of the two marbleized columns in the living room is structural, the other decorative. Comfortable furniture is covered in a variety of pale beige fabrics. By the window on the right is a Japanese puppet theater, on top of which is a Cambodian figure. Hanging above it is a Russian drinking horn. In front of the kitchen door at the back on the left is a zebra screen designed by Mark Hampton.

Hawkins's bedroom window overlooks the lake in Central Park. To the right can be seen the skyscrapers of midtown Manhattan, including the sloping roof of the Citicorp Building, and directly ahead, beyond the park, the apartment buildings on Fifth Avenue. (overleaf)

In this room cushions transform Hawkins's bed into a comfortable sofa by day. The wall color was based on the lining of one of his ties. On the right, a Tang dynasty camel with musicians stands on an unusual American Empire secretary. On the wall surrounding it are several nineteenth-century hand-colored lithographs of Egyptian monuments by David Roberts. On the wall to the left of the window is a Josef Albers painting and on the adjacent wall two Catlin hand-colored lithographs hang above a Van Day Truex drawing of the Circus Maximus.

which is easily converted into a comfortable sitting room. Brent Arnold helped to redesign this room and worked out the complex, saturated, ocher-and-brown-tinged gold of the walls, copied from the lining of one of Hawkins's ties. The art displayed in the bedroom is subdued, having to compete not only with the colored walls but also with the extraordinary views out of the unusually generous windows. To the east is a breathtaking panorama of Central Park. To the north, a stone's throw away at eye level are the neo-Gothic spires of William A. Potter's 1898 Universalist Church—once the Church of Divine Paternity.

In the bedroom, David Roberts's nineteenth-century views of Egypt are grouped together on one wall with a romantic nocturnal etching by Allen Blagdun of the actual view of the park from Hawkins's window. Dominating the wall is an unusual secretary. At first glance it seems to be a Biedermeier piece, but recent research suggests it was made in Pennsylvania in the 1830s, a time when the Empire style was going through a transitional phase. Its upper cabinet is cunningly fitted out with mirrors and columns, forming a quasi-hidden place to display small sculptures, and the writing desk has several secret drawers.

Another wall in the bedroom displays a significant work by Josef Albers. Done in 1947, it is perhaps one of his earliest variant paintings. A third wall holds a drawing by Van Day Truex, who ran the Parsons School of Design in Paris before World War II, and two Catlin hand-colored lithographs of

Indians, a wedding present from Hawkins's mother to his father. The large double bed is transformed by day into a deep sofa and loaded with cushions made from antique carpets. A coffee table has been devised from a piece of reverse painting on glass by Jean Du Pas—once part of the wall decoration in the dining saloon of the *Normandie*. A series of Brandt photographs of distorted nudes makes a bold statement. Near the bathroom door, which is partly concealed by a handsome mahogany, brass-hinged screen designed by Hampton, is a watercolor by Teddy Millington-Drake of a village on the island of Patmos, where Hawkins and the artist both have summer houses.

The bathroom is reached through a passage between clothing closets, which are screened by black-and-brown-printed cotton curtains. The bathroom window above the washbasin reveals another splendid view north. One wall has a cluster of George Platt Lynes photographs of the New York City Ballet's 1948 production of *Orpheus*, with sets and costumes by Noguchi. Once the usual shots had been taken, Lynes prevailed upon two members of the cast to redo their ballet poses in the nude. The ceiling has been painted by Alex Baker as a skyscape with the moon setting and sun rising, capturing the moment when both are clearly visible and in balance.

"You can have no idea the psychological lift this gives me every morning," Hawkins says, looking out at the view. "They really knew how to create views when they built this building."

CARNEGIE HILL TOWN HOUSE

Keeping track of Richard Jenrette's domiciles is no easy task. Since 1968, Jenrette, a founder of the investment banking firm of Donaldson, Lufkin & Jenrette and currently chairman of the board of the Equitable Life Assurance Society, has bought, restored, and painstakingly furnished sixteen dwellings. He currently owns Edgewater, a Greek Revival mansion on the Hudson River that once belonged to writer Gore Vidal (Jenrette is also chairman of Historic Hudson Valley); Ayr Mount, a grand house in North Carolina; Roper House on the Battery in Charleston, South Carolina; and Cane Garden, once a sugarcane plantation house in St. Croix, now filled with many local mahogany pieces. In addition, Mr. Jenrette has lived in various apartments, maisonettes, and town houses in different sections of New York City, furnishing them mostly with exemplary pieces of his favorite Federal and Empire styles.

Featured here is his house on Carnegie Hill. This area, the highest point in the city, encompasses 86th to 96th streets from Third to Fifth avenues. The hill was settled comparatively late in the city's history. For most of the nineteenth century goats roamed its sharp incline, so it was aptly dubbed Goat Hill. Old photographs show it devoid of houses—a scrubby, weed-scattered slope with a few ramshackle squatters' shacks.

Believing the higher the altitude, the healthier the air, industrialist Andrew Carnegie decided that his wife should live in the most elevated mansion in the city—though from all accounts she was a perfectly healthy woman. The neighborhood took its name from Carnegie's mansion, designed in 1901 by Babb, Cook & Willard. In 1977 it was renovated by Hardy Holzman Pfeiffer Associates and became the Cooper-Hewitt Museum, the Smith-

sonian Institution's National Museum of Design.

Nowadays the surrounding area is known for its abundance of private schools and museums. The latter include the Solomon R. Guggenheim Museum; the Museum of the City of New York; the National Academy of Design, which was once the Huntingtons' town house; the Jewish Museum; and the International Center for Photography. These, together with a number of other large mansions, have been the reason part of the neighborhood is now designated a historic district. Among the mansions are the Convent of the Sacred Heart, which was originally built for banker, philanthropist, and patron of the arts Otto Kahn in 1918; the Duchesne Residence School, built in 1902; the Consulate of the U.S.S.R., built in 1909 for John Henry Hammond; and the Smithers Alcoholism Center, Roosevelt Hospital, built in 1932. A few doors down from the Jenrette house is the Synod of Bishops of the Russian Orthodox Church outside of Russia, originally completed as a private house for Francis F. Palmer in 1917. Financier George F. Baker, Jr., later bought it and in 1928 added a ballroom designed by Delano & Aldrich.

Next door to the Baker mansion-turned-Russian-Orthodox-headquarters is another Baker adjunct—a garage with guest dwellings above, which was recently purchased by Richard Jenrette. And next to it is the Jenrette house shown here, which was designed for George Baker, Sr., in 1928, also by Delano & Aldrich. The senior Baker died in 1931 at the age of ninety-one but the house remained in family hands for another forty years.

Banker and philanthropist George F. Baker, Sr. (1840–1931), once president and chairman of the board of the First National Bank, which became the core of what is now Citibank, was an active member

The ceiling of the arch leading from the entrance hall into the stair hall was painted by Robert Jackson. The large, elaborately gilt-framed mirror in the stair hall belonged to the previous owner.

on the boards of no fewer than fifty major corporations, about one half of which were railroads. Self-described as "an old-fashioned banker," he was, despite his riches, a modest man. The house on 93rd Street next to his son's was built for his old age when he was infirm, and includes a "hidden" staircase leading to the room of his personal nurse, Helen Reddy.

When North Carolinian Richard Jenrette purchased the Baker house, his passion for rescuing "important" houses had become proverbial. He has been interested in houses, architecture, antique furniture, and paintings for the past twenty-five years. His name appears on Art & Antiques magazine's 100 Top Collectors list. His interest extends to his workplace: he has furnished the DLJ offices and more recently some of Equitable's offices with Duncan Phyfe and other classical furniture, and has been quoted as saying he believes that the early nineteenth century, when Phyfe flourished, was "a golden era, a period of great realism, and the last

flowering of hand-carved American furniture." He continues to believe that these pieces from America's early days as a republic are undervalued and unappreciated in comparison with furniture from the eighteenth-century Colonial period.

The front entrance of the Baker house on 93rd Street leads to a large marble-floored hall with a fireplace and two cloakrooms. An exemplary Duncan Phyfe sofa, originally owned by Governor De Witt Clinton and later by Berry Tracy, curator of the American Wing of the Metropolitan Museum, is the major piece of furniture here. Beyond the entrance hall is a stair hall that boasts a graceful elliptical stairway ascending through the four floors of the building to a skylight. Prints of an Indian tiger hunt bought at Rose Cummings's many years ago decorate a section of the walls of this hall.

One of the most beautiful rooms in the house is the oval dining room on the first floor beyond the hall. Three floor-to-ceiling windows face the small back garden. This room is graced with a marble

The oval dining room, with its elaborate and dramatic marble floor, is furnished with New York Federal dining room chairs. The Duncan Phyfe sideboard has much-sought-after furry-paw feet. Niches contain busts of Jefferson, Lafayette, John Paul Jones, and Robert Fulton. On the wall is a Gilbert Stuart portrait of Massachusetts governor and United States senator Edward Everett. The Regency chandelier from Nesle was selected because it replicated the decorative motif above the doorway.

The graceful spiral staircase ascends four floors from the street floor to a skylight. The stairs are covered in Scalamandré's coin-dotted dark green carpeting.

Original architectural details of the house included these built-in mahogany bookcases topped with marble urns in the niches above, which flank the arched window. The New York Duncan Phyfe sofa is covered in fabric from Scalamandré.

floor cunningly worked in an optical pattern. The yellow walls are decorated with marbleized pilasters punctuated by niches filled with copies of Houdon busts of American political leaders of the Revolutionary War period. A large butler's pantry, complete with silver safe and an old-fashioned pulley-system dumbwaiter, adjoins the dining room.

Much of the second floor is taken up with servants' quarters, offices, and workrooms, including a walk-in safe, trunk room, and two bathrooms. The floor above, the *piano nobile*, consists mainly of a large living room facing the street and Richard Jenrette's deep red office and study. The art in this room includes portraits of two former New York governors, De Witt Clinton and Daniel Tompkins, by Charles Willson Peale; a large portrait of Mr. Baker, for whom the house was built; and a set of architectural drawings by the architect Harold Sterner, including one of Edgewater. The top floor is the bedroom floor, with two bedrooms and a smaller study. A small staircase leads to a tiled roof terrace.

In the basement, the kitchen boasts extensive quarters befitting such a patrician house. A larder includes original gas-operated refrigerators and clothes dryers, though these are no longer hooked up for use. The original stove, however, still functions.

Throughout the house, the high-quality architectural details include original mahogany doors, silvered hardware, and a mahogany elevator. Richard Jenrette has maintained all these features and added his own touch to the house's authentic formality.

Though this kitchen has undergone partial renovation, the original stove is still in use. Off this room is a storage area, with the original gas-operated refrigerators, and a servants' dining room that has now been converted into a breakfast room.

The carpet in the large south-facing drawing room is a 1761 English needlepoint once used at Dumbarton Oaks in Washington, D.C. The secretary is from New York, circa 1820. On top is a bust of Judge William Gaston of North Carolina. The pair of portraits, by Gilbert Stuart (1755–1828), show General and Mrs. John Peter Van Ness. He became the first mayor of Washington, D.C., and she inherited most of what is now downtown Washington. The wood chairs and side tables are New York pieces. The damask-covered sofa and armchairs once belonged to Mrs. Robert Young, widow of the railroad tycoon.

In the master bedroom, the blue carpet decorated with gold wreaths and stars was designed by Bill Thompson. On the Federal four-poster is a coverlet of blue ottoman, with a gold-and-blue braid inset border. The swagged blue, cream, and yellow bed hangings are lined in cream sateen. Window curtains are of unlined, slubbed blue silk made with a pretty detail copied from Nancy Lancaster's room at Colefax & Fowler.

ACKNOWLEDGMENTS

This book would not have been possible without the cooperation of those who allowed us this glimpse into their private worlds. I would like to thank Anne H. Bass, Robert Brown, Simone di Bagno, Maxime de La Falaise, Mr. and Mrs. Edward Elliott Elson, Dean Fausett, Mr. and Mrs. Stephen Graham, Ashton Hawkins, Bryan Hunt, Richard Jenrette, John Kelley, Mr. and Mrs. Thomas Kempner, Gerald Keucher, Kenneth Jay Lane, Wade McCann, Barbara Munves, Mr. and Mrs. Eldo Netto, Frederick Norton, Dr. Judith Schneider and Norbert Weisburg, Sheila Shwartz and Irving Drabkin, Mr. and Mrs. Michael Somers, Mr. and Mrs. John Stubbs, Franklin Roosevelt Underwood, Timothy Van Dam, Ronald Wagner, the Rev. John Walsted, Hans Peter Weiss, Angus Wilkie, and Peri Wolfman and Charles Gold, as well as those who prefer to remain anonymous. I am grateful to those owners who not only took an interest in this book but also supplied invaluable information, showed patience with my endless questions, and offered generous advice. A special thanks goes to those whose residences came under consideration but, alas, do not appear in this book.

I am especially grateful for the help and encouragement of my agent and friend Angela Miller of Miller Press and her staff, including Sharon Squibb and Suzanne Dooley, who, during part of the time the book was being written, were with IMG Publishing. The enthusiasm and cooperation of everyone at Abbeville has been a joy, and of all the pleasant people there I would like to single out Abbeville's president, Robert Abrams; vice president Mark Magowan, my main liaison and smoother of many paths; Julie Rauer for her delightful design of the book; and extra special thanks to my editor, Jacqueline Decter, for her acumen, humor, and the pleasure of her company.

Alex McLean's talent and taste is obvious in his photographs. I am indebted to his congenial friendship during all our New York adventures. Thank you, Lizzie Himmel, for introducing us, and also for snapping us for the dust jacket! I'd also like to thank Bill Soyer, who steered me through the intimidating maze of word processing.

I am indebted to several authors who have covered New York's terrain in wonderful detail; in particular to Norval White and Elliot Willensky for the *AIA Guide* (New York Chapter, American Institute of Architects), which I found indispensable, accurate, and amusingly written. The same can be said for Paul Goldberger's witty *New York: The City Observed*. Thanks also go to Charles Lockwood for *Bricks and Brownstone: The New York Row House, 1783–1929*, to Barbaralee Diamondstein for *The Landmarks of New York*, and to Harmon H. Goldstone and Martha Dalrymple for *History Preserved: A Guide to New York City Landmarks and Historic Districts*. For help in my neighborhood libraries I'd like to mention Marilyn Schlansky and Virginia Sweeney of Reed Memorial Library, and Patricia Di Beradino at Patterson Library. And I'm grateful to the many efficient, dedicated librarians who aided me through countless hours of research—in particular those at the Local History and Genealogy room in New York's splendid public library at 42nd Street.

These remarkable residences could never have been photographed were it not for friends, aquaintances, and even strangers, who enthusiastically—and sometimes unwittingly—steered me in the right direction, gave information, or were in other ways most helpful. Among the many I would like to mention are Michael Adams, Marina Albee, Jeanne Atkinson, Stephen Barto, Richard Rodney Bennett, Lenore Benson, Jeffrey Bilhuber, Channing Blake, Max Bond, Lee Lee Brown, Walter Chatham, Professor John Henrik Clarke, Michael Crosbie, Catherine D'Alessio, Mme. Alexandra Danilova, Leamond Dean, Jacqueline Donnet, Catherine Eccles, Howard and Lou Erskine, Marilyn Evins, Georgina Fairholme, Ann Ferebee, Thomas J. Fleming, David Gibbons, Meredith Gladstone, Carla Glasser, Russell Glover, George Goodwill, Mark Hampton, Mary Ann Hannan, Gene Hovis, Edwin Jackson, William James, Doron Katzman, Max Kent, Gordon Knox, Caroline R. Lassoe, David McFadden, Patricia Gordon Michael, David Netto, Aaron Parker, David Piscuskas, Ted Porter, Jim Ray, Wilber Ross, Tom Seligson, Doris Shaw, Jeffrey Simpson, Richard Smith, Linda Stein, Ted Story, Bill Thompson, Peter Townsend, Lewis A. Ufland, Carol Volk, Dr. Ruth Westheimer, Thomas K. Woodward, and Thomas and Clelia Zacharias.

Most importantly, gratitude to my husband, Keith, and my daughters, Emma and Jassy, who have accepted the way I disappear into my writing room or chase off to look at other people's domiciles, often at the expense of ideal housekeeping in our own. I hope the end result shows my enthusiasm for this "best of all possible cities," for, no matter how you slice it, it's still the Big Apple.

SELECTED BIBLIOGRAPHY

BOOKS

Alpern, Andrew. *New York's Fabulous Luxury Apartments.* New York: Dover Publications, 1975.

Bryant, Beth. *The New Inside Guide to Greenwich Village.* New York: Oak Publications, 1965.

Delaney, Edmund T. *New York's Greenwich Village.* Barre, Mass.: Barre Publishers, 1968.

Diamondstein, Barbaralee. *The Landmarks of New York.* New York: Harry N. Abrams, 1988.

Garmey, Stephen. *Gramercy Park: An Illustrated History of a New York Neighborhood.* New York: Balsam Press, 1984.

Goldberger, Paul. *The City Observed: New York: A Guide to the Architecture of Manhattan.* New York: Vintage, 1979.

Goldstone, Harmon H., and Martha Dalrymple. *History Preserved: A Guide to New York City Landmarks and Historic Districts.* New York: Simon and Schuster, 1974.

Greenwich Village Historic District Designation Report, vol. 1. New York, 1969.

Lancaster, Clay. *Old Brooklyn Heights: New York's First Suburb.* New York: Dover Publications, 1979.

Lanier, Henry Wynsham. *Greenwich Village: Today and Yesterday.* New York: Harper and Brothers, 1949.

Lockwood, Charles. *Bricks and Brownstone: The New York Row House, 1783–1929.* New York: Abbeville Press, 1972.

Logan, Sheridan A. *George F. Baker: His Bank, 1840–1955.* St. Joseph, Mo.: Stinehour Press and Meriden Gravure Company, 1981.

McCullough, David. *Brooklyn . . . And How It Got That Way.* New York: Dial Press, 1983.

McDarrah, Fred. *Greenwich Village.* New York: Corinth Books, 1963.

Moscow, Henry. *The Street Book; An Encyclopedia of Manhattan's Street Names and Their Origins.* New York: Hagstrom, 1979.

Niles, Bo. *White by Design.* New York: Stewart, Tabori and Chang, 1984.

Shackleton, Robert. *The Book of New York.* Philadelphia: Penn Publishing Company, 1917.

Simon, Kate. *Fifth Avenue: A Very Social History.* New York: Harcourt Brace Jovanovich, 1978.

Thornton, Peter. *Authentic Décor: The Domestic Interior, 1620–1920.* London: Weidenfeld & Nicolson, 1984.

Ware, Caroline. *Greenwich Village: 1920–1930.* Boston: Houghton Mifflin, 1935. Reprint. New York: Octagon, 1977.

White, Noral, and Elliot Willensky. *AIA Guide to New York City.* New York: Collier Macmillan, 1978.

Wilkie, Angus. *Biedermeier.* New York: Abbeville Press, 1987.

PAMPHLETS AND PERIODICALS

"Clinton Hill, Brooklyn." Pamphlet produced by the Society for Clinton Hill in conjunction with the Brooklyn Museum and the Brooklyn Educational and Cultural Alliance.

"Clinton Hill Homes' '84 Tour." Pamphlet and poster produced by the Society for Clinton Hill, Brooklyn, 1984.

Duggin, Charles. "How to Build Your Country Houses," *Horticulturalist,* 1862.

Gray, Christopher. "Apartments by Candela: Grandest of the Grand," *New York Times,* January 1989.

Heilpern, John. "The Bass Reserve," *Vogue,* December 1988, pp. 344–353.

The Hill: Neighborhood News of Clinton Hill, Fort Greene, and Wallabout (May–June 1984).

Koenig, Rhoda. "A La Falaise," *HG* 160 (September 1988): 192–203, 236, 238.

Kornbluth, Jesse. "A Gallery of His Own," *House & Garden* 156 (July 1984): 100–105.

Ludwig, James W. "Alphabet of Greatness: Manhattan's Street Names." New York Public Library, 1961. Typescript.